# The Disappearance of Jimmy Hoffa

Pete Bird

Published by Trellis Publishing, 2021.

While every precaution has been taken in the preparation of this book, the publisher assumes no responsibility for errors or omissions, or for damages resulting from the use of the information contained herein.

THE DISAPPEARANCE OF JIMMY HOFFA

**First edition. July 5, 2021.**

Copyright © 2021 Pete Bird.

ISBN: 979-8224173242

Written by Pete Bird.

# THE DISAPPEARANCE OF JIMMY HOFFA

PETE DOVE

**Jimmy Hoffa – The More We Hear, The Less We Understand**

'The Irishman' is a great film. OK, so at almost three and a half hours running time it's a tad on the long side. But with stars like Al Pacino, Joe Pesci and Robert De Niro working under the direction of Martin Scorsese, those hours are bound to pass quickly, and with, if not exactly enjoyment (it's not that kind of film), then certainly plenty of interest.

Indeed, there are many who believe that its multiple Oscar nominations – nine in total – should have translated into at least three or four of the rolls-of-film-podiumed statues. But for all the qualities of the movie, we should not lose sight that its primary purpose is as a piece of public entertainment. In terms of relating the true story of Jimmy Hoffa, some of its story lines can be taken with a liberal pinch of salt.

Hoffa's paternal predecessors can be traced back to Germany, before they emigrated to join the largish group of Europeans who settled in Pennsylvania. The Hoffa line moved East to Indiana in the mid-1800s. His mother's side were also immigrants, some of the many who made the journey across the Atlantic from Ireland.

Jimmy was born on Valentine's day 1913 in the small town of Brazil, Clay County which lies in the east of the state of Indiana. It is not the most salubrious of cities. Named after a farm in the area (the owner of which called his own homestead after the country in the mid-1800s), it is the poorest in Indiana, with almost a third of its population living below the poverty line.

Back in the early years of the twentieth century Brazil was no different. Many of its struggling inhabitants were coal miners, subject to the risks and hazards of that dangerous profession. Jimmy was just seven when his father, John, who worked as a driller in the choking pits, died from lung disease almost certainly caused by his employment. Naturally, the notions of health and safety, compensations and insurances were little more than fantastical dreams for the impoverished of Clay County, and the family were left destitute.

Mom Viola was not one to feel sorry for herself, however. 'She believed that Duty and Discipline were spelled with capital Ds' said Jimmy sometime later about his resolute mother. She started to work in a local laundry, and her meagre income from that was supplemented as Jimmy and his three siblings worked after school jobs to earn a few dollars. This was a family determined to survive. So, when Viola heard about the manufacturing opportunities for those prepared to work hard that existed in the tough city of Detroit, she upped sticks and took the entire family there. It was 1924, and Jimmy was eleven years old.

Despite a promising academic career at school, he knew that family came first and aged fourteen he dropped out of education in order to work full time to support, and indeed protect, his family. But having lost his father to industrial insouciance, and with a mother dedicated to hard work and mutual support, it was inevitable that the rights of the workers should matter to him. They did, from the outset. His first full time job became the final piece of that particular jigsaw.

The short but stockily built young Jimmy Hoffa was required to work twelve-hour shifts loading and unloading grocery products from railway trucks. The pay was atrocious, with money earned only being paid for the actual goods moved, not for the long hours of the shift. Kroger's grocery chain may well be a respectable company these days, one which pays its employees a proper wage and which adheres to proper health and safety laws. But times were different then, ninety years ago. And so, probably, was the Kroger grocery company.

Despite his youthfulness, Jimmy began to be recognised by the tough men in the yard, who were impressed by his determination, his bravery and his organisational skills. He was offered a key role in the union, and soon the grocery workers were on strike. The campaign was successful, and the workers saw their contracts improved.

This was a remarkable achievement. The late twenties and early thirties were a time of enormous financial uncertainty in the US. Employers were ready to hire gangs of thugs to break up strikes, and union men were a ready target for frequently violent assault. Yet this young lad stood strong and tall, and achieved his goals.

It got him noticed and in 1932 he left the grocery company and accepted the offer of a role as an organiser for the Teamsters Local 299, based in Detroit.

'Let each member do his duty as he sees fit. Let each put his shoulder to the wheel and work together to bring about better results. Let no member sow the seeds of discourse within our ranks...' the philosophy of the Teamsters is one that would sit well with an idealistic youngster like Jimmy. It is certainly worth noting that the General President of the Teamsters today is one James P Hoffa; the son of Jimmy. He is the second longest serving post holder in the one hundred- and seventeen-year history of the union, and has been elected five times to the position, which he has held since 1998.

Union business runs in the family.

Hoffa was a fine union leader. In the beginning, at least. One of his tasks was to strengthen the collective might of the Teamsters. He was hugely successful in this. The union had 75000 members in 1933; by 1939 that number had swelled to 420,000. By six years after the end of World War II, that figure had risen to over a million. The Teamsters were now one of the most powerful unions in the USA, at a time when one in three workers belonged to such an organisation.

Hoffa developed a highly effective strategy to support his workers' aims. He employed strikes on the hoof, calling men out at a moment's notice. The strategy created mayhem in management plans, and once the union became large enough that if could not be bullied into submission, led to deals favourable to the striking workers.

He also operated a policy of secondary boycotts, where one union would support the interests of another, and this collective approach further strengthened the Teamsters' power. Hoffa became a household name, a working-class hero to many. In a strangely seditious way, a marker for the American dream. The USA was a place where anybody could make good. Look at Jimmy Hoffa. A man who started with nothing and was now one of the most powerful men in industry.

But there was a downside. Teamsters were unions which particularly catered for men and, later, women who worked in warehouses, and in commercial transport. That meant trucks. And truck unions had established a line of command of their own. A particularly unpleasant one. Because many such unions had links to, and were often controlled by, organised crime syndicates. Hoffa needed to make a choice. He could leave these unions as independent bodies, relatively small and organisations which largely served as convenient money laundering centres for gangsters, or he could bring them together, and enhance their power.

He chose the latter option, and in doing so came to the conclusion that he could not smash the syndicates that held such influence over these unions; instead, he would work with them. When war broke out, like many, he faced being drafted and shipped overseas. But Jimmy had influence now, even though he was only in his late twenties. He was able to make the case that by remaining in the US and continuing his work as a union leader, he would contribute far more to the war effort than by being sent to fight, and possibly die, in Europe or the Far East. His influence could keep freight moving, and in doing so that would be a major benefit to the war effort. Maybe.

It was a sign of the increasing political skills Hoffa was developing. By the early 1950s, as we have seen, the Teamsters (or IBT, international brotherhood of teamsters, to give them their full name) had become incredibly powerful. Daniel Tobin had been president of the organisation pretty much since its inception. Now, more than forty years on, it was time for a change. Dave Beck, a Master of Political shenanigans himself, was to be the new incumbent. A role he secured very much thanks to work behind the scenes carried out by Hoffa. There had been an internal revolt in the union against Tobin, and this had been quelled by securing support from the Central States for his planned successor, Beck. The man who had weaved his way through this minefield was Jimmy Hoffa. He got his reward, with Beck appointing him vice president of the Teamsters.

As it got bigger, so the union became increasingly political. It set up its headquarters away from Indianapolis, and to the very centre of political power and influence – Washington DC. With so many uncertain deals taking place, and the influence on the union of organised crime growing, it seemed, exponentially, Hoffa decided he needed his own personal lawyer. Just for protection. The man he chose was Bill Bufalino.

On the face of it, Bufalino seems to come from an immaculate pedigree. He was a lieutenant in the army, a member of the Judge Advocate General Corps where he served in World War II. He spent time studying to become a Roman Catholic priest.

Then, in 1942, he found his niche and became a lawyer, qualifying from the Dickinson School of Law in Carlisle, Pennsylvania. But these admirable career choices hide the truth, or at least, a significant part of it. In 1945 he met, fell in love with and quickly married Antoinette Meli. Her uncle was the Detroit crime boss, Angelo Meli.

'In the underworld,' Bufalino said later, 'you either have to be born in it or you have to get in by marriage...I married a Detroit girl.' Bufalino always denied any connections to the Mob. However, there is evidence suggesting the contrary. He began a Jukebox business when such a field was highly lucrative. But he needed cash to get the business up and running. $100000 from his wife's uncle along with another uncertain character, John Priziola, and others, set him on his way. The Bilvin Distributing Company was up and running; jukeboxes were a handy field, because the delivery and maintenance systems for these technological wonders of their day lay in the hands, in Detroit at least, of the Meli family.

Bufalino's claim that he avoided the criminal underworld might not stand up to scrutiny; FBI sources described him as a 'made man' thanks to his dodgy connections. But the idea that he was not born into a criminal family also faltered under close examination. His cousin was a mightily powerful Pennsylvanian Godfather, Russell Bufalino. Later, Bill Bufalino would make his cousin's Godfather status legitimate, by asking him to perform that role to his own daughter.

The two were more than cousins. Bill Bufalino once said: 'If you want to charge me with something regarding Russell Bufalino, charge me with the fact that I selected him as my number one friend...This is a closer relationship than a brother.'

Bufalino had secured a post as president of a branch of the Teamsters, the Local 985, which happened to oversee Detroit's Jukebox business. It ran this for more than twenty years. During those years he employed his considerable skills as a lawyer to fight the Teamster cause in the court, winning five of seven trials they encountered.

Meanwhile Jimmy Hoffa was feeling the pressure. Becoming increasingly more hot tempered and unpredictable, he started to establish closer connections to organised crime in Pennsylvania. The police began to cast their eyes in his direction, especially regarding racketeering. It seemed as though, having sought to get the mob onside to further his union's cause, now he was becoming indebted to them. Having a powerful and at least semi legitimate face such as Hoffa's to front some of their more audacious activities was appealing to the Mob, and Hoffa, it appeared, was always ready to oblige.

Bill Bufalino said later of his friend: 'There'll never be another one like that in the Teamsters. If he was a woman, he'd be pregnant every nine months. He didn't know how to say no. He did so many favours for so many people.'

With pressure mounting on him from all sides, legal and otherwise, Hoffa needed a reliable and well-connected personal lawyer. The morally loose Bufalino had the expertise and the family to perform that role.

It is a sign of the important role Jimmy Hoffa had taken in industrial relations that he came to the notice of the powerful Kennedy clan – a family never far from controversy themselves, of course. Robert Kennedy, younger brother to future President John F, was a counsel to the McClellan Committee which had sought to bring the union boss down. That select committee was convened to look at improper activities in Labor and Management.

The story which attracted the attention of Kennedy is a complex one. But one significant in Hoffa's life story. In 1955, Hoffa had begun an attempt to usurp Dave Beck as the Chairman of the Teamsters. The story goes that he had enlisted the help of a mobster, Johnny Dio, and together they created fifteen fake locals, paper unions whose membership amounted to precisely zero, but whose pretend populous could be counted on to put their imaginary weight behind Hoffa's campaign.

Problems escalated inevitably and rapidly, and by the following year matters had come under the nose of McLellan's investigation – at that stage a member of the subcommittee responsible for Government operations. Such was the influence of Hoffa that he managed to get the matter reviewed under the senate's Labor Committee only, where John F Kennedy held sway. A known supporter of the unions, his investigation went skin deep at best. The result of this complete horlicks was the creation of Labor and Management committee. From that moment on, Hoffa became a marked man.

Whilst, astonishingly, he was acquitted of any wrongdoing in this vote rigging exercise (evidence of the power of the mob and the influence Hoffa wielded) any breathing space was short-lived. After his election victory, JFK appointed his brother, Robert, as Attorney General and gave the green light for a stinging and far reaching assault on organised crime. At the heart of his zealous campaign lay the 'Get Hoffa' squad, a collection of hard-hitting prosecutors and single-minded investigators who were determined to allow Robert

Kennedy to succeed where he had failed before and bring down the diminutive union man. Indictments for jury tampering followed, but Hoffa had a strong popular following, and the Government simply could not make its charges stick.

But 1964 would prove to be the year his luck turned, when the tide of affairs of union matter finally began to overwhelm Hoffa. In March of that year he found himself once more before the courts, this time facing charges of bribery of a grand juror. These related to another legal battle he had encountered in 1962, when he had faced a conspiracy trial, but had withstood the allegations thrown at him.

But now, though, his good fortune ran out. On March 4th, in Chattanooga, Tennessee, the express train of the law ran him down. He was sentenced to eight years imprisonment and a fine of $10000 for his actions in bribing the juror.

He immediately appealed and found himself free but on bail. By 26th July he had been convicted once again, this time for conspiracy, mail fraud and wire fraud to gain improper use of the Teamsters' pension fund. It is hard not to see the influence of the organised crime syndicates as being the ones ultimately behind this scandal. Now, it was an additional five years behind bars on his slate. Hoffa spent the following three years appealing these convictions with ever increasing desperation. At one stage, his defense attorney managed to get his clients convictions reviewed at the Supreme Court.

This determined lawyer was Morris Shenker, a man who, it appeared, enjoyed as shady a life as Bill Bufalino. Shenker had arrived in the US in 1922. He was a Russian Jew who found himself in St Louis, and his poor English was not allowed to stand in his way. He became a successful lawyer, studying at the Washington University School of Law, and was soon gaining a name as a go-to defence attorney.

But by the time he was working for Hoffa, his ties to the underworld were becoming a concern. He was exposed in a report in Life Magazine in 1970 of having 'personal ties to the underworld', and that indeed it was he who controlled the huge, three quarters of a billion dollars Teamsters Union Pension Fund. He got into the casino world dominated by organised crime syndicates in the early 1970s, although failed to gain a foothold here.

During that decade, he became increasingly in debt to the pension funds for which he had oversight, borrowing over $200 million for his various, usually unsuccessful, enterprises. By the mid-1980s he was out of money and filed for Bankruptcy after one of the unions he had fleeced, the Culinary Workers, succeeded in gaining a court judgement for the $34 million he had 'borrowed' from them. He would undoubtedly have faced trial, but ill health intervened, and he was never prosecuted.

Hoffa certainly knew how to pick his defense teams.

But his appeals and challenges finally ran out and in 1967 he began a 13-year sentence for his two convictions.

He served under a third of his time. The reason for that was the intervention of another role model of American public life, Richard Nixon. He pardoned Hoffa in 1971, placing as a condition that the union man should stay out of union business until 1980. It might have seemed a good deal. By now Hoffa was 58, an age when most are beginning to think about slowing down. He had a good reputation among his followers and was still loved by his old union membership. Money would never be a problem for him.

From Nixon's side, there were many potential advantages to be gained from such a move. It is more than possible that the disgraced Republican enjoyed his own ties to organised crime. Freeing Hoffa would, on the face of it, seem to strengthen his position with these underworld operators. More likely is that pardoning Hoffa would win him support among the Teamster membership. In those days it was unthinkable that a major union would get behind a Republican candidate. But the Teamsters did. They provided financial support to Nixon's 1972 re-election campaign; it is believed. Payments that were clandestine in nature. Further monies washed into various accounts which are thought to have been used by Nixon and his team when Watergate began to pollute the waters of his political life.

There are more who believe that Nixon's cronies used some Teamster's members as a kind of private army to bully and harass political opponents. Another theory is that by releasing Hoffa, the Teamsters would be indebted to Nixon, and he could then influence them to ensure that there was no solid wall of union opposition to his presidency.

Nixon's major mistake, however, was that he underestimated Hoffa's passion for his union. Even while inside the Teamster's chairman was plotting how he could regain his seat of power. Once on the loose, these meanderings took on an even more directed path.

It was while Hoffa was inside serving his time that his relationship with Bill Bufalino finally came to an end. 'I went to see him every week until we came to the point that every time, he was dissatisfied with something, he had to have somebody to blame,' the lawyer claimed.

The truth was probably more complicated. Inside prison Hoffa had time to think, to review his life. His passion had always been the union and supporting the rights of the men and women who belonged to the Teamsters. Yes, he had enjoyed the benefits of close association with the mob, but this was a by-product, something he was able to portray to his own conscience as a necessary evil in his journey to promote the union.

To Hoffa's thinking, it was not his fault if the truck drivers' unions held long established links to organised crime. Further, his connections had not enabled him to stay out of prison. When he did leave, he was determined to return to his union activities. That became his focus, and in becoming so his loyalty to the Pennsylvania and Detroit mobsters began to erode.

Bufalino, for his part, somehow managed to keep the balance between being a part of the family, so to speak, and avoiding prosecution for his nefarious actions. Indeed, he frequently claimed that he never broke any laws. Now he had to make a choice. Did he stick with his friend, or his family? Really, given the nature of that family, there was never ever a genuine doubt. Blood is thicker than water, especially when that blood is tainted by the mob.

It is now, with Hoffa released from jail. that we return to Martin Scorsese's blockbuster, The Irishman. Or, more particularly the role of Hoffa's long-time friend and mob associate, Frank Sheeran, who was known as 'the Irishman' and is played with startling menace by Robert De Niro in the film. Allegedly, the story of the final years of Hoffa's life goes as follows.

On his release from prison, Hoffa immediately began to seek ways to get back into the Union world, even though this was in a direct breach of the conditions for his pardon. To have any chance of success, he would have to turn his back on the families of the mob whom he had served, and been supported by, for years.

Frank Sheeran was a union man himself, and an enforcer. A hired thug who would do his bosses' bidding however extreme those instructions might be. As he allowed distance to grow between himself and the mobsters, Hoffa's standing with the underworld mafia began to crumble. Old grievances came to the fore; Hoffa had been well looked after, now he was being ungrateful. His new interests were disrespectful to the leaders of the families who controlled the unions he wished to lead again.

According to Charles Brandt, who was Sheeran's lawyer and became the author of his top selling memoirs 'I Hear You Paint Houses' (apparently, Hoffa's theatrically threatening yet ambiguous comment to the 'Irishman' when he met him for the first time). In it there are even suggestions that the mob were claiming that they had indeed been involved in supplying the gun which killed John F Kennedy in Dallas. Ostensibly, the story says, that had been a favour for Hoffa, and now he was not being grateful enough for the deed. 'I realised he was talking about the assassination of President Kennedy in 1963,' claimed

Brandt about the incident. 'It was always rumoured that the killer, Lee Harvey Oswald, wasn't working alone and that the mob was behind it.' Conspiracy theorists were wetting themselves with delight up and down the country when that particular gem made it to the newspapers.

Matters became more and more heated, and on 30th July 1975 two mafia dons summoned Hoffa to a meeting at a secret house. Later, his car was found outside a Detroit Restaurant, but Hoffa was never seen again.

Sheeran claims he picked up the union man, by now in his sixties, from the restaurant. He knew that the former leader would not have got in the car with any other hoodlums, such as the two who were accompanying him, but that he would trust Sheeran.

Then, at the house, he allowed himself to fall a little behind Hoffa as they made their way inside. There, he shot Hoffa in the back of the head, killing him. Sheeran claims to have dropped hints to his friend, encouraging him not to attend the meeting, but when Hoffa decided to go ahead, he had no choice but to carry out his murderous orders.

'Hoffa was Sheeran's friend, but you didn't defy orders,' Brandt explained. 'If he hadn't killed him, he'd have been shot himself.' Allegedly, Hoffa's body was transferred to a mob run crematorium, where it was hidden forever, in the best way possible.

The only problem with the story, other than it really does seem like the plot for a B list gangster movie of the 1940s, is that it is almost certainly not true. Sheeran, it is widely claimed, exaggerated his friendship with Hoffa. It is hard to believe that anybody other than the Mafia executed Hoffa – he knew too much about their activities to be allowed to live while apparently growing apart from their influence. But while Sheeran might have been present or heard about the plans to kill his not quite as close as he claimed friend, there is little evidence to suggest he did it. Possibly, some blood stains later revealed might have indicated that somebody, at one time, was seriously injured – maybe killed – in the house to which Sheeran led his author. But he was close to death at this time, ravaged by cancer, and desperate to leave his mark on history.

Despite the power of The Irishman's story, the brilliance of its lead performers and its persuasive presentation, the fact remains that nobody is really any closer to knowing the truth about Jimmy Hoffa's demise today than they were approaching half a century ago.

# STALKED & ABDUCTED : THE TRUE STORY OF BRIANNA MAITLAND

## KENDRA HICKS

There are approximately 2,300 United States citizens reported missing every single day. Some of these are runaways, some are misunderstandings, some are hurt or killed, and other just disappear without a trace. The friends and families they left behind are left with just a glimmer of hope that their loved one may one day turn up, which is oftentimes more painful than the closure of knowing your child or friend is in a better place.

Missing persons cases are a popular subject matter for shows like Criminal Minds or CSI: Crime Scene Investigation, but many real life cases don't end in the happily-ever-after seen on primetime. In the real world, these cases are often full of loose and dead ends, muddied by apathetic law enforcement or unclear communication between the victim and those close to them. Of those that go missing, the majority are women, who often present themselves as an easy target for those looking to inflict harm on another.

On March 19th, 2004, Brianna Maitland disappeared. The 17-year-old girl had just left the Black Lantern Inn in Montgomery, Vermont, where she washed dishes and occasionally served tables, when her car was found abandoned only twenty minutes later. Despite a brief visit from a local police officer, and curious passersby photographing the abandoned Oldsmobile, she was not reported missing for several days. Her parents, Bruce and Kelli Maitland, assumed she was at home, and Brianna's roommate was out of town at the time. Brianna left a trail of clues behind her, but over 12 years later there is still no official story for what happened that night. As the years pass without any major leads, the investigation has petered out and will soon be coming to a close.

**Who Was Brianna Maitland?**

Brianna Maitland was born and raised in Burlington, Vermont, where she spent the first seventeen years of her life living at her parents' quiet farmhouse. On her seventeenth birthday, she packed up her belongings and moved out on her own, despite her parent's pleas for her to stay another year. Her mother told interviewers that there was no serious issue or conflict that resulted in this decision, but that her daughter was fiercely independent and prematurely ready to venture into the world on her own. Although Brianna's early departure caused many to suspect an unhappy childhood or home life, she and her parents appeared to maintain a good, somewhat close relationship for the months after her move.

Brianna was an attractive girl, easily looking several years older than her young age. She was brunette and slightly petite, at 5 foot 4 inches and about one hundred and ten pounds. All around, she seemed to be a well-liked girl with many friends. Some rumors emerged after her disappearance regarding her moving to a new school district. These rumors blamed the move on Brianna being bullied relentlessly by other girls at her original high school, which motivated Brianna to pick up and move her life to an entirely different area. While these rumors are persistent, Brianna's parents or friends haven't confirmed them at this point.

At first, Brianna moved in with her boyfriend, James, wanting to be closer to a group of her friends that lived over 15 miles away from her parents' community. Moving in with her then-boyfriend seemed to be more a move of convenience than love; it didn't appear that she moved out of her parents' house with the intent of being closer and more codependent with him. She enrolled in a new high school, the same one as these friends, and began to settle into her new living situation. Unfortunately, her new home life was quickly uprooted by arguments with James, who she had accused in letters of having a severe drinking problem. By February 2004, barely a month before she would disappear without a trace, Brianna had dropped out of school and moved to a new house.

Now living with Jillian Stout, a friend she had known since early childhood, Brianna attempted to regain control of her life. The two young girls shared a modest home in Sheldon, Vermont, and seemed to be doing fairly well for themselves. Brianna enrolled herself in a high school equivalency program, hoping to earn her G.E.D. as soon as she would have earned her high school diploma if she had not dropped out. Brianna was reportedly excited about this test, looking forward to a new chapter of her newly independent life. Despite the hardships she had fallen on after moving from her parent's house, Brianna was determined to pull herself up and support herself on her own. Sadly, she would disappear only hours after finishing her exam.

While Brianna was not known as a serious troublemaker, she did drink and party like so many other teenagers do. At one of these parties, only three weeks before the night of her disappearance, Brianna was assaulted by another girl from her high school. At the hands of this girl, named Keallie Lacross, Brianna suffered a broken nose and concussion. Some rumors surrounding this attack suggest that Kaellie or one of her friends felt threatened by the pretty Brianna when she was seen talking to their boyfriend or a boy they were interested in. Although Brianna did press legal charges against Keallie, these were not yet resolved when she disappeared, so they were dropped several weeks later.

This scene cast light on some of the darker sides of Brianna's life. Her boyfriend was likely and alcoholic if not worse, she was bullied and harassed by other girls in her social circle who disliked her, and she likely partook in drugs and alcohol herself. While this isn't unusual for a 17-year-old, many in the community and police force expressed doubt that Brianna was attacked or hurt in some way. Instead, to them, she was just another burnt out, teenage runaway.

### The Morning of Her Disappearance

The morning of Brianna's G.E.D. examination, she and her mother, Kellie Maitland, met for breakfast. Kellie reported that there was nothing out of the ordinary at this time, and that she had sent her daughter off to her test with plans to meet up and celebrate with her later.

For her celebration, Brianna chose to go shopping with her mother in the afternoon. Kellie said that shopping was one of her daughter's absolute favorite things to do. She said Brianna could walk into any store, pick the most "avant gard" piece off the rack, and model it like she was on an international runway. Brianna's sense of style was something her mother and many others admired about her. In television and print interviews, Kellie Maitland retells these memories with a clear fondness, holding onto those last final hours she spent with her daughter in 2004.

However, according to her mother, Brianna's shopping trip was cut short. As they were waiting in line to check out at one of her favorite stores, Kellie said that Brianna's attention was caught by something outside the store window. Saying that she would be right back, Brianna left the store. Kellie is unsure where he daughter actually went; she said that she never saw Brianna enter another storefront on the street. After paying for her items, Kellie exited the store and found Brianna waiting for her at their vehicle. She had no shopping bag from another store with her, and there was no one else nearby that Kellie thought she could have been speaking to.

There are many speculations as to what, or who, drew Brianna Maitland out of the store that morning. No matter what happened, Kellie said that her daughter was visibly upset the entire car-ride home. Wanting to respect her daughter's privacy, Kellie never asked Brianna what had happened earlier that afternoon, but this would be the last time she ever spoke to her beloved daughter. She dropped Brianna off in the driveway of her and Jillian's shared house, and then turned onto the highway to the quiet farmhouse she and Brianna had once both called home.

At home, Briana started getting ready for her Friday night shift at the Black Lantern Inn, one of the teenager's two minimum wage jobs. At around 3:30 in the afternoon, Brianna left her house in her 1985 Oldsmobile, leaving a note for Jillian assuring her that she would be back home after her shift was over. Jillian found the note when she arrived home, after Brianna had already left for the Inn, but then went away for the weekend without ever hearing from Brianna again.

**The Last Known Sighting**

The Black Lantern Inn, founded in 1803, closed its doors for good on March 29th, 2015. Remnants of the Inn's events and menus can still be found on Facebook and outdated travel sites. The most recent post on the Black Lantern Inn's Facebook page simply says, "The Black Lantern Inn is closed." The Inn offered an Irish restaurant and brewpub, which featured the Inn's own small batch beer brewed on location. Located in Montgomery, Vermont, a small town nestled between the East Coast's rolling mountains, the Black Lantern Inn drew a combination of loyal locals and transient tourists to its establishment. With a fireplace and public house feel, the restaurant and brewpub offered a cozy retreat for the perfect stag night or romantic getaway on a cold winter night. This is where Brianna Maitland spent her last documented hours.

Friday nights are notoriously busy in the restaurant and service industry, and March 19th, 2004, was no exception. In fact, it was even busier than expected, keeping the staff on their feet for the better part of the night and filling the back of house with dirty dishes and utensils. Backed up on her work, Brianna stayed several hours later than usual in order to finish washing the entirety of the night's dishes.

Sometime during the evening, Kellie and Bruce Maitland passed the Black Lantern Inn, hoping to stop in and visit Brianna at her new workplace. However, after seeing how busy the restaurant was, and not wanting to embarrass their daughter in front of her coworkers and boss, they continued on their way home. To this day, Kellie regrets not making that stop, if only to see her daughter one last time.

At 11:20 that night, the Inn's staff members were finally done with all of their closing duties. As per restaurant tradition, they all planned to hang out, have a drink, and relax after a hard night's work. Brianna, however, declined, stating that she needed to get to bed in time for her Saturday morning shift at her other job in nearby St. Albans, Vermont.

As far as Brianna's coworkers reported, she left alone from the Black Lantern Inn in her usual ride, her mother's hand-me-down Oldsmobile sedan. Brianna and Jillian's home was about twenty miles outside of Montgomery, but Brianna's vehicle didn't make it further than a mile from the Black Lantern Inn. And, as far as anyone knows, perhaps neither did Brianna.

Shortly after 11:30 that night, a man driving down Route 118 reported seeing a seemingly empty car parked at a run-down building, known as "the old Dutchburn house." He said the headlights were on, but he didn't notice anyone inside or near the exterior of the vehicle. A little after midnight, another report came in of a stopped car at the Dutchburn house, this time with a turn signal on. Later in the night, at about 4 a.m., an ex-boyfriend of Brianna Maitland noticed the vehicle parked off the road as well. Finally, early the next morning, a group of travelers stopped to examine the oddly abandoned vehicle, even going so far as to take photographs of the unusual scene.

**A Delayed Investigation**

Daylight revealed that the vehicle had actually been backed into the Dutchburn house, damaging the wooden exterior. By early afternoon on March 20th, a Vermont State Police officer finally arrived at the scene, deeming the car abandoned and having it towed to a local salvage lot. It wouldn't be until March 25th that the oddly abandoned car would be identified as Brianna's Oldsmobile.

Because of a series of unfortunate circumstances, no one noticed Brianna's absence until Tuesday, the 23rd, when Jillian called Kellie Maitland to ask if she had heard from Brianna. Since she was away all weekend, Jillian just assumed that Brianna had made other plans and had simply not returned home yet. It is unknown why her second job, which she was scheduled to work Saturday morning, did not question her absence. It's possible that they just thought she was another teenager pulling a no-call-no-show, too apathetic to formally quit.

As soon as Kellie heard that her daughter had been missing for several days, she began calling everyone she could think of. Despite trying to contact her friends, employers, and other family, Kellie failed to find any information on where Brianna could be. With no leads to go off of, she called the local police to file a missing persons report.

At this point, Brianna's Oldsmobile had been removed from the Dutchburn house almost five days ago. That Thursday, March 25th, Kellie and Bruce drove to the Vermont State Police in St. Albans to submit photos of Brianna with her report. It was then that an officer showed them the photos of the abandoned Oldsmobile on Route 118, and the Maitland's identified the vehicle as Brianna's.

As the news of Brianna's disappearance broke, questions began to emerge as to why the officer sent to investigate the Oldsmobile had not raised an earlier alarm. The Oldsmobile had been littered with all kinds of Brianna's personal belongs both within and outside of the vehicle, including: two uncashed paychecks, her purse, jewelry, spare change, a water bottle, and, perhaps strangest of all, a lime slice. Vomit, assumed to belong to Brianna, was also found in the car's front seat. News articles, personal bloggers, and other armchair detectives have accused the officer, seemingly unnamed in any public documents, of complete negligence when handling the Brianna Maitland case.

While the Vermont State Police conducted a several month long investigation, they held onto the belief that there was no foul play involved in Brianna's disappearance. The general consensus was that she had run away or been swept up in some kind of substance abuse. Brianna's friends and family continue to believe that she would not abandon her life and belongings like that.

In 2012, a young woman's skull was found on a Vermont highway, showing signs of age and being exposed to the elements for several years. While no conclusive evidence has been able to tie this discovery to Brianna or one of the other missing women in Vermont, it remains a possible sign of her fate.

Recently, on the twelfth anniversary of Brianna's disappearance, law enforcement revealed that they had collected DNA evidence from inside the abandoned Oldsmobile. It is unknown if this DNA solely belonged to Brianna, or if this was new evidence or had been collected during the initial investigation. There have been no public updates related to this potentially new evidence.

Brianna's family maintains a Facebook page dedicated to remembering her and encouraging others to come forward with information about her or other missing persons. Support for Brianna and her family continues to flow in through comments and pictures posted to the page.

**Flurry of Theories**

Unsolved mysteries, whether they be in the form of everyday murder or the paranormal, are a popular pastime for the average armchair detective. Brianna Maitland's case is no exception. There is no limit to the number of rumors and theories built up around her disappearance, some more believable than others. While there is no official statement on what actually happened to Brianna at this time, by breaking down the most prominent theories we can begin to understand what might have happened that night. While this list is not inclusive of every theory about Brianna's disappearance, it features the most likely or those that are most supported by the case's evidence.

**A Drug Deal Gone Bad** – One of the more common theories regarding Brianna's disappearance connects the scene of her abandoned car with the shopping incident reported by her mother. It is known that, like many girls her age, Brianna was often seen at parties where alcohol and other substances were being used. Whether Brianna had an issue with any particular drug is unknown, but it's very likely that she partook at least occasionally, and she regular hung out with teenagers who were known drug users and dealers. These facts lead many people, including some police officers, to believe that Brianna was caught up in a bad drug deal or otherwise got on the bad side of some of the area's dealers.

The most common story within this theory is that Brianna owed money to a local cocaine dealer, who she had been avoiding for some time. When out shopping with her mother earlier on the day of her disappearance, Brianna had spotted this dealer or one of their associates following her and her mother around town. This is when Brianna had gone outside, confronting the dealer and possibly promising to meet him later on with the money he was owed.

Later that night, either because the dealer was simply sick of waiting for his money or because Brianna attempted to avoid him once more, things turned violent. What happened after Brianna's car was abandoned is not entirely answered by this particular theory, but it is clear serious harm was done to Brianna Maitland that night or shortly after. Later, a story would emerge that filled out some of this theory's more gruesome details.

**Murdered by Ramon Ryans** – About three years after Brianna's disappearance, a police report from the Burlington Police Department offered to potentially solve the mystery. This report, given by Debbie Gorton, from Colchester, Vermont, claimed to answer the questions that the Maitland family and law enforcement had been asking for years.

Gorton's statement came about because her sister, Ellen Ducharme, had been charged with the drug-related murder of Ligia Collins. Some speculate that this story was an attempt to throw attention off of Gorton's son, who had recently been arrested for an unrelated crime, but that question remains unanswered.

In Gorton's statement, she claimed that Ducharme had told her about the murder and disposal of Brianna, committed by Ducharme and several of her associates. According to Ducharme, a known drug dealer, named Ramon Ryans, had taken a "couple thousand" dollars from Brianna which she had given him to buy crack cocaine. Brianna, either because she decided she needed the money for something else or because Ryans failed to deliver on the deal, confronted Ryans to ask for her money back. Ducharme told Gorton that Ryans had abducted Brianna on the night of March 19th, when her car was found abandoned.

Ducharme told Burlington police that Brianna was kept alive for up to a week, suffering who knows what kind of emotional and physical abuse at the hands of Ryans and his friends. Brianna was kept in Ryans basement, possibly even past the time of her death. According to Ducharme, Briann's body was dumped at an unknown local pig farm.

It is particularly strange, if this is truly what happened, why Brianna's attackers did not take her money or un-cashed paychecks from her vehicle. If her murder was motivated by money, these would be easy loot. More likely, though, this was a crime of pure rage.

Gorton believed that several people were involved in the murder and disposal of Brianna's body, including her sister, Ramon Ryans, Moses Robar, Darrel Robar, and Timothy Crews. No charges were ever made against these individuals in the case of Brianna's disappearance and the accusations remain uncorroborated by any local law enforcement.

**Stalked at Work** – It is sadly common for service industry staff, especially women, to be harassed and followed by their customers. While Brianna's primary role was in the back as a dishwasher, she occasionally served and helped out in the front of house when it was busy.

Another common theory of her disappearance is that she had acquired a stalker in her time at the restaurant, or from somewhere else who had then found her workplace and continued his stalking there. Since Brianna was an attractive, young girl, this theory is not too hard to believe.

Perhaps Brianna was aware of this stalker, though never confided in the police or her loved ones, and this is who she had seen outside the store she was shopping in with her mother. If she had confronted this man and demanded that he leave her alone, this would have made her nervous and on-edge like her mother later described. This rejection by his object of affection may have also sent the stalker into more violent methods.

With this theory, some believe that the man was hiding in her Oldsmobile's backseat, waiting for Brianna to clock out and head home. Shortly after she had left the Black Lantern Inn, he could have emerged and told her to either pull over or drive somewhere at his command. This also would have explained why the Oldsmobile was backed into the old Dutchburn house, because oftentimes women are instructed to drive into an object in order to stun or hurt an attacker in their vehicle. Unfortunately, if this is what happened, it appears that the stalker was successful in his pursuit of Brianna.

**Pregnancy Scare** – Fueled by the small town rumor mill, another frequently heard story is one of teenage pregnancy. Playing up Brianna's partying side, this theory suggests that a mistake between two young people turned into a case of cold-blooded murder.

On the day of her disappearance, Brianna already knew that she was pregnant. Maybe she had just found out, or maybe this fact had been weighing on her mind for weeks. Either way, when she left her mother in the store checkout line, Brianna was going out to tell someone about her pregnancy. Whether this was a friend or the potential child's father, Brianna did not want her mother to overhear the conversation and find out that she was pregnant.

Later that night, she had stopped at the old Dutchburn house. The vomit found in her vehicle leads some to believe that she got sick on her way home from work and pulled over in order to clean up or gather herself before continuing home. This is where someone met her, because she asked him or her to or because they had followed her from the Black Lantern Inn, most likely the potential child's father. Either way, this person was extremely unhappy at Brianna's news. Perhaps it was a cheating partner who had gotten Brianna pregnant, or simply a young man who was nowhere near ready for the financial and emotional responsibility of having a child.

The old Dutchburn house is backed by a nearby forest and river, which can be easily accessed by a short walk. If Brianna was killed at the location of her car, this is likely where her body was left. No trace of Brianna was ever found in this area, but there is always a chance that it was swept away or buried beneath the soil.

**A Deadly Party** – Following along with Brianna's supposed party girl image, this theory suggested that she had actually made it further than the old Dutchburn house that night. However, as we'll see, there are some discrepancies throughout this theory that make it highly unlikely.

After leaving for work that Friday, rather than going home to rest for her morning shift like she had told her coworkers, Brianna had driven out to a nearby party. Here she was either involuntarily drugged or willing took drugs herself. As the night progressed and intoxication levels increased, Brianna began to overdose. Unable or unwilling to get her the appropriate help in time, Brianna died that night at the party. Afraid of being caught, and potentially charged with the murder of Brianna, those at the party secretly disposed of the body. Later that night, her car was planted in order to look like it had been abandoned or that something had happened to her on the side of the road. If a couple drunk teenagers were driving Brianna's vehicle to the old Dutchburn house, this could also explain the vomit found in the passenger seat of her car.

The most obvious hole in this theory is the sightings of Brianna's parked car at the Dutchburn house less than an hour after she had clocked out of work at the Black Lantern Inn. This timeframe would leave her no time to get to a party, let alone overdose and have her vehicle planted by other partygoers. However, witness sightings are notoriously inaccurate, leading some to believe that the initial sighting of Brianna's Oldsmobile either didn't happen, was a different car pulled over on the side of the road entirely, or happened at a later hour and the witness was either mistaken or lied to the authorities.

For those who see Brianna as a wild, high school drop out who ended up hanging out with the wrong crowd, this story might be very easy to believe. Even law enforcement were quick to say that Brianna's disappearance was more likely an accident than premeditated foul play. Brianna's close friends and family don't believe this tale, though, and hold onto the belief that Brianna was an innocent victim the night of her disappearance.

**A Victim of Human Trafficking** – Human trafficking is an often overlooked issue in the United States, with many believing that it only occurs in foreign, third world countries in Asia or Europe. While most known cases of human trafficking occur at airports, large metropolitan areas, and other locations with a high volume of travellers and business, some do occur in small towns or seemingly innocuous places like coffee shops or malls.

Women are the most common victims of human trafficking, usually being sold into the non-consensual sex trade. While the men, or "Johns," who visit these women are rarely aware that the sex worker they are visiting is actually being held against their will, these women's captors can be violent, abusive, and frequently end up killings their prisoners. Some human traffickers will also force their victims to develop a drug addiction, often to heroin and other hard street drugs, so that they are more easily manipulated and apathetic to their situation.

Those who believe that Brianna, likely targeted because of her petite, non-threatening figure and good looks, was sold into sex trafficking believe that she was smuggled over the nearby Canadian border. This would explain why her personal belongings, such as I.D.

and jewelry, were left behind; the abductors would not want any identifiable information with her in case they were caught. However, it's strange that none of her money was taken if this was the case.

**Final Blow From Kaellie Lacross** – While Kaellie Lacross's, the girl who had attacked Brianna at a party just three weeks before her disappearance, charges were eventually dropped, she remained the primary suspect in many people's eyes. After all, it is quite possible that a grudge strong enough to assault someone over is a grudge strong enough to murder someone, purposely or not, over.

Whatever it is that triggered Kaellie's attack at the party, it's not impossible to believe that she wasn't satisfied with the outcome. If Kaellie was intending to teach Brianna a lesson, whether it was to not speak poorly or her or to stay away from particular boy, she might have felt the need to scare Brianna even further. Knowing that Brianna worked at the Black Lantern Inn, Kaellie could have followed her and forced her to pull over on the side of Route 118.

Here, Kaellie, likely the help of her peers, could have threatened Brianna and physically attacked her again. Whether this attack was meant to kill Brianna doesn't matter, only that it eventually did. Realizing that they had made a huge mistake, and would now be charged with not just assault but with murder as well, the group quickly disposed of her body. They could have placed the body in another vehicle, taking it to a different location, or carried her back into the secluded woods behind the old Dutchburn house.

If the motivation behind this attack was only to scare Brianna, then they would have had no interest in taking her money or other belongings. This theory is supported by having a clear motive, though there is no official report on what the conflict between Brianna and Kaellie was, and if it was serious enough that Kaellie would gone through the trouble of practically hunting Brianna down to resolve it.

**The Mystery Remains**

Despite this exhaustive list of theories, there is really no way of knowing what happened to Brianna until someone comes forward with new information. As the Maitland family and Montgomery community approach the thirteenth anniversary of Brianna's disappearance, there are plans to scale back the search for her and what happened.

Up until now, the Maitland family and Vermont State Police have funded a $20,000 reward fund for any information that leads to the discovery of Brianna Maitland, but after all these years with no solid leads, the plan is to donate the fund to a missing persons advocacy group sometime in 2017. Although the Maitland's have not given up hope, they are ready to take a step forward in grieving their daughter, no matter what has happened to her.

The Brianna Maitland Facebook page remains active, wishing followers happy holidays and posting alerts for other missing persons cases. Serving as a memory of Brianna, whether she remains alive or not, the page aims to draw out information on her case and the thousands of other missing persons cases that go unsolved every year. Brianna's case has also been featured on several true crime podcasts, television shows, and blogs, hoping to unearth the answers to questions that everyone has been asking since that cold night of March 19th, 2004.

# THE DISAPPEARANCE OF KELSIE SCHELLING

# ANA BENSON

Every time a woman goes missing or is found murdered, the police usually takes a closer look at their spouses or boyfriends. It is a standard procedure, especially if there were indications that they were in a troubled relationship. The disappearance of Kelsie Schelling is one of the biggest mysteries in Colorado. This young pregnant woman was last seen in February of 2013 and the case is still open to this day.

However, Kelsie's family was quite disappointed at the lack of interest by the police to investigate her then-boyfriend Donthe Lucas, who was clearly involved in this crime. After all, Donthe did invite Kelsie to his hometown on that fateful night and he was the last person who saw her alive. When they realized that the police are stalling with the investigation, the family made a promise that Kelsie's case will not be forgotten until they discover what really happened. They kept the public informed through their Facebook page and eventually managed to reach the Colorado Bureau of Investigation.

Early life

Kelsie Jean Schelling was born on 18th February 1991 in Holyoke, Colorado. She grew up in a tightknit family and later became even closer to her mother after the divorce of her parents. Kelsie was only eleven years old when they split up but she would often talk to her father as well. However, they didn't see each other that often because he moved to a different part of town. After graduating from high school, Kelsie attended Northeastern Junior College located in Sterling, Colorado. She was fascinated with psychology and planned to major in it once she gets accepted to the university.

Kelsie was friendly and outspoken, so it comes as no surprise that she had many friends and was a life of every party. During her time at Northeastern Junior College, Kelsie met Donthe Lucas. He was a star player on the basketball team and the two of them fell in love instantly. Donthe Lucas had a very difficult childhood and he grew up in Pueblo, Colorado which is an infamous place known for higher crime rates than anywhere else in the state. He loved basketball and it was clear that he would be an outstanding athlete even in high school. Basketball players do have enormous salaries so Donthe Lucas did see it as an opportunity to help his family out further down the line.

He was hoping that a scout would attend one of his games and recruit him for one of bigger colleges or universities that had a good basketball team. But his big break never happened. Instead, he ended up in Northeastern Junior College which was alright, but Donthe wasn't quite happy with that outcome. His dissatisfaction was evident even in the relationship with Kelsie. Their romance had constant ups and downs, and the two of them would break up, and get back together which drove Kelsie mad. They did finally call it quits after several semesters, and didn't see each other for quite some time.

After finishing the two years at the junior college, Kelsie pursued her education even further, and she moved to California to attend Vanguard University in Costa Mesa. She was finally able to study psychology full time. Donthe continued to play basketball for Emporia State University in Kansas. Kelsie's family was happy she managed to end her relationship with the troubled basketball player, and they hoped that she would make a new life far away from Colorado. Kelsie was independent and she enjoyed living and studying in California. When she wasn't attending classes, Kelsie worked at a tanning salon with her best friend. However, she did drop out of the college because the school work was a bit too much for her at the time and her only option was to go back home. She moved to Denver in 2012 and started working in a store. Meanwhile, Donthe Lucas was back in his hometown Pueblo.

The two of them started talking once again during the autumn of 2012. It was obvious that they still had feelings for each other, so no one was surprised when Donthe and Kelsie decided to spend the Christmas holidays together. The couple seemed happy to everyone around them, but Kelsie did tell her friends that their relationship was still very toxic. Donthe was still treating her badly, calling her names, and starting unnecessary fights. Soon enough everything will change. A few weeks after the holidays, Kelsie found out that she was pregnant. Shocked at first, Kelsie was lost and decided not to tell anyone for a couple of weeks. But keeping a secret was hard. So she called her mother and told her the news. Kelsie's mother Laura would later say that even though her daughter felt a bit stressed, she was still excited about the pregnancy. Yes, she was young but Kelsie was determined to make it work.

Donthe Lucas didn't take the news so well. Having in mind how dissatisfied he felt about his failed basketball career, it is not wrong to assume that the news about a baby simply solidified the fact that his dreams will never come true. Kelsie noticed the change in his mood and openly told him that he doesn't have to be a part of their baby's life. But it is also worth mentioning that Kelsie confided in her best friend that Donthe was ecstatic to become a father at one point. However, his mind was constantly changing. Kelsie went to see her doctor on 4th of February 2013 and he confirmed that she was eight weeks pregnant. The baby was healthy and doing well. The doctor provided her with an ultrasound of the unborn baby, and she was full of joy. Kelsie immediately sent out the pictures to her mother, her friends, and Donthe. Unfortunately, the excitement will not last forever.

The night of the disappearance

Donthe and Kelsey exchanged several emails on February 3rd, 2013. He invited her to visit him in Pueblo. She turned him down saying that she needs to go for a checkup the next day to make sure everything is alright with the baby. After seeing her doctor on the morning of February 4th, 2013, Kelsie went straight to the store. She worked the second shift and was expected to come home sometime after 10:00 PM that night. However, she was in contact with Donthe for the entire day, texting back and forth about the pregnancy. Donthe told her that she should drive out to Pueblo after work because he had a surprise for her. Not knowing what it is, Kelsie asked for more information because Pueblo is two hours away from Denver, and she would probably be tired after work. He insisted that she would be happy with his surprise and that he cannot tell her anything over the phone.

It is safe to assume that Kelsie thought that Donthe was ready to change and start a family with her. Their relationship wasn't a standard one but it seemed like Kelsie was willing to move past all the negative things and focus on the future. So after her shift ended, Kelsie got in her Chevy Cruze LTZ and drove to Pueblo in the middle of the night. Donthe was supposed to meet her in a parking lot in front of a local Walmart. The surveillance cameras did confirm that Kelsie got there on time, but Donthe was nowhere to be seen. She waited in a parked car for almost an hour before sending another text message to Donthe, saying that she has been in the parking lot for too long and that she would come pick him up at whatever location he is at the moment. She got a reply sometime around 12:15 AM.

Donthe told her that he will be waiting for her in the street next to his grandmother's home. Kelsie is seen exiting the parking lot a couple of minutes after she got the message. She clearly did arrive at the second rendezvous spot, but once again Donthe wasn't there. Kelsie sent him another message asking where is he and Donthe replied that he will be there in a minute. This is the last known communication between these two until sometime before 04:00 AM. After going through the phone records, police did discover that Donthe called Kelsie at 03:54 AM but she didn't pick up. The significance of this mysterious phone call will be revealed later. After reviewing the cell tower pings for both phones, the investigators did discover that they were in close proximity to each other.

The search for Kelsie

Kelsie's mother Laura got really worried the next day because she wasn't able to reach her daughter over the phone. She tried calling numerous times but it went straight to the voicemail. The last message she got from her daughter was the ultrasound image of her unborn child, and Laura wasn't sure if something happened to Kelsie after work, or she was ignoring her calls. Laura contacted Kelsie's friends who told her that she went to Pueblo to meet with Donthe. With no word from her daughter, she called Donthe who picked up his phone and told Laura that he had seen Kelsie last night, but that she drove back home in the morning.

Laura was starting to panic, but she did tell Donthe that she would involve the police if she doesn't hear from her daughter soon. Laura and Kelsie were very close and they did tell each other everything, but she suspected that her daughter kept this information from her because she didn't want Laura to know that she was meeting with Donthe. After all, Laura was aware of the nature of their relationship, and his reluctance to accept the baby. Plus, Laura would probably advise Kelsie not to go to Pueblo in the middle of the night.

Laura contacted the local law enforcement and told them that her daughter was missing. Without any solid leads or evidence, they started asking around for Kelsie. Their first step was to take a closer look at Donthe because he claimed that he was the last person to saw Kelsie. She did travel from Denver just to see him. After checking Kelsie's credit card records, they did notice that the card was used hours after Kelsie's last known contact with Donthe. They reviewed the surveillance of the ATM and noticed that Donthe had the card and picked up $400 from Kelsie's account. They weren't sure if Donthe had Kelsie's agreement to use the card, but that was a felony in the state of Colorado, so he was led to the police station for questioning. He had a lot of things to clear up, starting with the timeline of Kelsie's visit to Pueblo.

Donthe's interview

After being picked up by the police, Donthe told his own version of the story. They did see each other that night and talked until early morning hours. Donthe and Kelsie got into a fight and she felt too agitated to drive back home to Denver. She was also very tired from working the second shift. Instead, Kelsie decided to sleep in her car which was parked near his grandmother's house. According to Donthe, his phone rang sometime around 07:00 AM and it was Kelsie. She wasn't feeling well and asked Donthe to drive her to a hospital. He put on his clothes, got to her car, and drove her to the Parkview Hospital.

Kelsie wasn't sure if something happened to the baby during their argument last night and she insisted to see a doctor before she heads out to Denver. Donthe sat inside her car in the parking lot for two hours when she finally emerged from the hospital. Kelsie told him that she had lost the baby. She then asked Donthe to drive her to Walmart to get something to eat and buy some snacks for the road. The two of them started fighting while they were in Walmart and Kelsie refused to drive him home. Donthe simply walked away and got to his grandmother's house on foot. He didn't see Kelsie later in the day and he assumed she went home. He didn't mention stopping at the ATM to pick up the money during his initial interview.

The investigators did notice a couple of possible leads that could collaborate Donthe's story, namely the Parkview Hospital. Each medical facility keeps detailed records of the patients they treat. After speaking to the staff and going through the data, they have confirmed that Kelsie didn't check in during the morning of February 5th. There were also numerous surveillance cameras all over the building and none of them picked up Kelsie entering or leaving the hospital. It was obvious that this part of Donthe's story was not true.

Of course, the police investigators decided to check out Walmart as well because the parking lot and stores do have surveillance cameras, and they might have picked up something that would be of use. While they couldn't find Kelsie or Donthe entering the Walmart, they did notice Kelsie's car on the parking lot. However, the timeline didn't match up with Donthe's story because Kelsie's car appeared at noon, and not in the morning. Plus, Donthe was the only passenger in the car.

Another surveillance camera which was positioned on the back side of Walmart did record Donthe getting into his mother's car – another detail he failed to mention in the initial talk with the investigators.

Without any proof that Donthe's version of the events is true, they called him up for a second interview. The investigators did have a plan this time - they wanted to find out more about the ATM, and how it fits into his timeline. He told the detectives that he took $400 in order to pay his bills and that Kelsie lent him the money since he was at the ATM while Kelsie was at the hospital. When the detectives told Donthe that there is no record of Kelsie ever being in that hospital, his reply was: "I don't even know what to say right now."

They also presented him with Walmart surveillance video that proves Donthe was the only person in the car. He was surprised with the evidence put in front of him, and before the detectives managed to get him to open up, he decided to lawyer up. He was only charged with the identity theft due to the fact that he used Kelsie's credit card, but the case was dropped. The judge had determined that Donthe did use Kelsie's credit card in the past and it was a normal behavior. However, nobody managed to figure out why Donthe had her card in the first place. After all, if Kelsie decided to ran away and start a new life, she would need the money, as well as her vehicle.

Speaking of Kelsie's car, the investigators took a closer look at the surveillance video from Walmart parking lot because they wanted to follow the vehicle. Exactly one day after Donthe left Kelsie's car there, another man approached the car and got inside by using the key. He didn't break in or steal the car. The man was dressed in black, wearing a hoodie, so identifying him was almost impossible. His body type was different than Donthe's, and the mystery man was significantly shorter. Keep in mind that Donthe was a tall basketball player, so his height would be noticeable, even in a low-quality video.

Seeing the direction in which the car went, the police collected the surveillance videos from stores and businesses which were in close proximity. They put the puzzle pieces together and found a route but they couldn't follow it all the way. One day later, the car was dropped at the parking lot of Saint Mary Corwin Hospital. The man locked the car and walked away. The investigators located the vehicle on 14th of February, 2013 and figured out the timeline. But nobody knows where the car was during 6th of February. There weren't any signs of a struggle that would indicate that Kelsie was killed in her car. Almost all of her personal items were missing, including her wallet and a backpack.

While it is unclear if the vehicle was tested for the traces of DNA, an unnamed police officer who worked for Pueblo Police Department will later say that they did find bodily fluids in the trunk of Kelsie's car, as well as two palm prints. However, no one knows what happened with this evidence and was it ever tested. It is simply another thing which the police investigators decided to ignore in this case. Unfortunately, the whole investigation will be under scrutiny soon after.

Theories

Figuring out a solid theory without too many evidence or information can be challenging. Laura, Kelsie's mother, claims that her daughter was probably murdered and that it was premeditated. The first red flag for her was Donthe's initial invitation to meet him before the doctor's appointment. When Kelsie refused, he knew that he had to act fast. Donthe lured Kelsie to Pueblo by saying that he has something to show her, but he never gave an explanation to the law enforcement about what the surprise really was.

It is clear that Kelsie was alive and well up until the point she met Donthe in the street next to his grandmother's house. This is where the trail goes cold. The activity on her phone stops until 04:00 AM. If we analyze the location of the phones, another theory is that Donthe led Kelsie to a remote location and harmed her. It was possible that Kelsie dropped her phone in the middle of a struggle. Donthe couldn't find the phone in the dark, so he had to call her number. He was very likely getting rid of the evidence.

There is a possibility that the two of them did indeed get into a fight, and that an unfortunate accident happened. However, it is more likely that Donthe planned to get rid of Kelsie, and had planned every single step he would take that night. He really insisted to see her as soon as possible. While it is not fair to put the blame on the rest of Lucas family, the fact that his mother picked him up immediately after he left Kelsie's vehicle at the Walmart's parking lot indicates that she knew what was going on. Pueblo Police Department did stop investigating Donthe, and they claimed they didn't have enough physical evidence to prove that a crime really occurred. But they did receive a couple of noteworthy tips which were ignored and never pursued.

The missed opportunities

The entire investigation of the disappearance of Kelsie Schelling was troubling from the very beginning. While the detectives did not have physical evidence of a crime, it was clear that Donthe was the last person who saw Kelsie alive. In every standard investigation, he would have been the prime suspect, and the investigators would do their best to find more proof that he was somehow connected to the crime. The cell tower pings did show that both of their phones were in a remote area next to Pueblo in the early morning hours.

But there are even bigger missed opportunities that could have provided the investigators with the proof they needed. For instance, Donthe was living in his grandmother's house at the time of Kelsie's disappearance. However, the entire family moved out soon after. The landlord started redecorating the house because he wanted to rent it again. He did hear about the missing girl from Denver but had no idea about the details of the case, or the fact that the Lucas family was involved in any way.

He decided to put the new carpets in and when he lifted the old one, the landlord noticed a strange stain on the bottom. He contacted the police enforcement because he was worried that something bad has happened in the house. However, the police ignored his request to check out the stained carpet, and no one had ever arrived at Lucas' previous residence to pick it up. The landlord ended up throwing the carpet away because he simply couldn't keep it forever in the house and wanted to move on with the renovation.

Another missed opportunity involved a couple of fishermen who were out on a lake on a night fishing expedition. It is important to mention that the lake was located near the Saint Mary Corwin Hospital. As you might recall, that was the spot where the police officers discovered Kelsie's vehicle on the 14th of February 2013. They were out on a bank when a hook got stuck to something poking out of the sand. The fishermen went to investigate and were sure that they saw a part of a human ribcage, as well as a skull.

They were terrified by that discovery and left the area right away. Both of them were reluctant to notify the police because they did have some troubles with the law in the past. But that didn't stop them from telling this story to their friends who urged them to contact the local law enforcement. A couple of months passed before they finally talked to the police, but the lake wasn't searched afterward.

The current searches

Family and friends continued to search for Kelsie even after it was clear that the police enforcement forgot about her case. They created a Facebook group that was constantly updated with new information. Pueblo Police Department did go through many changes after Kelsie went missing. The lead investigator was replaced with a new one who was willing to cooperate with the Schelling family. The Schellings did offer a large reward for any new leads that might help them locate their missing daughter. The reward was $100,000 at one point.

This eventually led to false claims and misleading messages such as the one which claimed that Kelsie was still alive, but was placed into a sex traffic ring after a hired hitman decided not to kill her.

Laura Schelling contacted the police and told them about the message. Since the investigators decided to follow every lead possible, they dug deeper and even involved the FBI. Their experts did manage to trace the message back to Russia through the IP address so it was clear that this tip was useless.

The biggest break in the case happened in the spring of 2017 when Colorado Bureau of Investigation finally got the authorization from the local law enforcement to join the search. CBI did determine that the prime suspect should be Donthe Lucas, and they got the warrant to search the area around his previous place of residence. A large number of police officers was seen around that house during April of 2017, and they dug up the parts of the backyard using heavy machinery.

The search has been successful and the officers left the scene carrying bags of evidence. However, they stated that they didn't find any traces of Kelsie's remains. Kelsie's family released the following statement after the search: "The past 2 days have been grueling and emotional, ending with the outcome we did not hope for. Kelsie is still missing. There is no way for me to convey to you all the pain that I feel right now. Sincere, heartfelt thanks goes out to the members of Pueblo PD, CBI and Parks & Rec who worked so hard on this search for Kelsie. This was a physically demanding excavation for them and we witnessed how hard they worked. Despite all the issues we have had in the past, the new leadership over Kelsie's case from PPD and active involvement from CBI is giving us hope that an effective investigation is finally taking place."

The case is still active and the police didn't arrest Donthe. But the positive changes are happening and Kelsie's family is certain that they will find the answers they are looking for now that the investigation is finally moving forward.

# THE DISAPPEARANCE OF BRITTANEE DREXEL

43

## FAITH TORINO

Brittanee Drexel disappeared from Myrtle Beach, SC while on spring break on April 25, 2009. She was 17 at the time and traveled without receiving parental consent. She told her mother that she was staying at a friend's house near their home in Rochester, New York. Brittanee's mother, Dawn, then learned where she really was when her boyfriend, John, called her after he suspected something had happened to Brittanee. Her parents immediately grew angry, scared, and devastated when they received word that their daughter was missing.

Brittanee was born on October 7th, 1991 and lived in Rochester, New York. She moved frequently during her youth as her father was in the military. She was a junior at Gates-Chili High school and the year was a rough one with her parents separating. She would live with her mother but still see her father frequently.

She was blind in her right eye and had several surgeries to correct her hyperplastic primary vitreous. To keep her eye from wandering, she would get contacts that made both eyes look the same.

Britt was described by friends and family as a smiling, fun-loving girl. Her demeanor had changed by her junior year in high school as she was depressed that her parents were separating. She would sleep in late and begin to skip school. She would overdose two times on her mother's pain medication and both times were fueled by the fact that she had just broken up with her on-again, off-again boyfriend, John Grieco.

"I felt it was all my fault," Brittany's father said. "When I was here none of this went on. She didn't ingest as many pills as they thought but still watching her get her stomach pumped was a warning. I need help."

"I remember the look on her face," Dawn said. "She was all red. She was crying, tears coming down her face. 'Why would you do this? Nothing in life is that bad.'"

Brittanee would be forced to see a counselor after the suicide attempt. Still, things seemed as if they were a mess on the home front.

Her parents were separating and her mother was losing her home. But she would resume her studies at school and excel on the soccer field.

"She was fast," her father said. "Her coach would say he'd never seen a girl that fast."

By the time Spring Break rolled around in, she was ready to go on an adventure with some of the older kids she knew. It was a long-standing tradition for Rochester students to go to Myrtle Beach for vacation. Britt wanted to enjoy the night life and lay out in the beach, so when one of her older friends asked if she wanted to come along she didn't hesitate.

She asked her mother first and the idea was immediately shot dawn. Dawn Drexel did not know any of the friends that would be taking Brittanee.

"She asked me and I said 'no,'" Dawn recalled. "Then she went to talk to her father. She would play us both. She would say Mom said 'no' but Dad said 'yes.'"

Brittanee was determined to go. She pleaded with her mother once again and was turned down. Angry, the two got into a fight and Britt would call her boyfriend to come pick her up.

Brittanee decided to fool her mother. She told her mother that she wanted to stay at a friend's house nearby for a couple of days. Dawn reluctantly agreed but Brittanee headed off to South Carolina instead.

Dawn believed that someone had offered her something, like a "modeling job or some other kind of ruse" to get her to go down there. She had aspirations of being a model as well as getting into cosmetology. With her striking good looks, she would be a shoo-in for success in the modeling profession.

"Her biological father was Turkish," Dawn said. "She had a very European look."

Defying her mother, Brittanee would visit her boyfriend at his workplace and tried to entice him to come along. The young man declined, stating that he had to work.

Brittanee then left with her older friends Jennifer Oberer, Phillip Oberer and Allana Lippa to Myrtle Beach. Jennifer was twenty-one years old. Her brother Phillip would be charged with rape in an unrelated case (charges would be dropped) in 2010. It is believed that these were considered the 'cool kids' and that Britt wanted to hang out and be liked by them.

Britt texted her boyfriend numerous times throughout the trip, telling him about the ambience. She expressed her love for the hot weather, palm trees and the happy vibe of young people finally away from parental supervision. But according to friends and family, Brittanee didn't know the older kids that well.

She also called her mother and lied, telling her that she waswatching movies at a friend's house.

CHANGE OF HEART

Britt hit the clubs with her friends and her mood quickly changed. Her friends began using a lot of drugs and she didn't want any part of that scene. She went off by herself, checking out the local shops and walking down the beach.

She then met up with a friend from Rochester, a man named Peter Brozowitz. He was also in town and staying at the Blue Water Resort with his own group of friends; Matthew Abrams, Philip Watson, Keith Cummings, and Anthony Schimizzi. The 20-year old Brozowitz was a "club promoter" who got Brittanee into Club Kryptonite. The next morning, she would meet Peter again at the beach.

The next day, Brittanee called her younger sister and told her that she's at the beach. Her sister believed she's at the local beach which is only twenty-minutes away. Britt then has a friend to impersonate the parent of the friend get on the phone to talk to her mother. The friend assured Dawn that everything was okay.

Britt then got back on the phone with her mother.

"I'll see you tomorrow," Britt said. "I love you and I'll see you tomorrow."

It would be the last time Dawn would ever speak to her daughter.

## THE MYSTERY OF WHAT HAPPENED THAT NIGHT

Brittanee decided she would meet up with her friend Peter that night. She borrowed a pair of shorts from a friend and headed out. She texted her boyfriend John, telling him that she's having a miserable time and that she doesn't like the people she went down with. Apparently, they were 'mean-girling' her after she didn't do drugs with them.

She then received a text from her friend who stated that she wants her shorts back. Irritated, Brittanee walked back to the hotel to return the item.

At least that is what her friends say happened as Britt would disappear into the night.

John then became worried when Britt did not text him back. He texted her a few more times, waited, received no answer then he threatened to tell her mother that she's in South Carolina if she doesn't respond back.

Convinced that something is wrong, John calls Dawn at home. He explained that Brittanee is in Myrtle Beach.

Dawn went livid but her anger soon turned to concern when Britt didn't respond to her own texts or calls.

Everyone in Brittanee's family was notified. Something was wrong. Terribly wrong.

The next morning Dawn, her parents and John all made the trek to Myrtle Beach to try and look for Brittanee.

## THE SEARCH BEGINS

Police in Myrtle Beach were notified and questioned the friends that Britt had been staying with. Their answers were all the same, they had not seen Brittanee since last night. Police also turned to Dawn, questioning her about Brittanee's state of mind.

Would she run away? Had she done this before?

There was no indication that Brittanee had motivation to do such a thing. Nor did they have any reason to believe she was doing a lot of drinking or drugs.

With no other leads, detectives turned their eyes on the last person to have seen Brittanee, Peter Brozovitz.

Peter would make an appearance on the Dr.Phil show and proclaim his innocence. He stated that they were in his hotel room watching the Yankees-Red Sox game when Brittanee was engaged in a texting argument with Jen Oberer who wanted her shorts back.

He said she didn't have a problem with walking a mile back to her own hotel.

Brittanee's parents were on the show and berated Peter for not "being a gentleman" and driving her back to the hotel. They also found it suspicious that Peter and the rest of Brittanee's friends did not do more after she was missing.

"I had spoken with Peter that morning," Dawn said. "He was giving me three different scenarios...It's fishy."

Peter responded angrily, stating that he was 'being thrown under the bus.' The innuendos were clear, that even if he had nothing to do with Brittanee's disappearance, she went missing because he didn't look out for her.

What is suspicious is that Peter had abruptly left Myrtle Beach with his friends around 2 a.m, five hours after Brittanee had vanished. They left clothing behind in their hotel room and looked to have been in a rush.

Upon his return to Rochester, Peter hired a defense attorney.

Peter had told investigators that she left his room shortly upon arrival to return the pair of shorts to her friend. The detectives got a hold of the surveillance camera from the hotel and verified Peter's story. At precisely 8:48 that evening she was seen leaving Peter's hotel to return back to her own hotel. She should have shown up on a traffic camera about fifteen minutes away but she never made it that far. She was abducted somewhere along that street.

Police continued to question Peter. The young man stated that one of his friends was told by his mother to return home immediately. This story was corroborated and law enforcement did not pursue the matter any further.

Instead, they now focused on Britt's cell phone.

Britt's last text message to her boyfriend was around 8:58. Ten minutes after she had left the hotel she texted "I'm packing and going to sleep probably."

This would be the last outbound message she sent as then John began texting her repeatedly with no answer back.

But the calls she received from John and her friends were pinged by her cell phone. Every time a friend called, her cell phone communicated with the nearest tower.

In looking at her cell phone records, she was moving southbound. The last ping was received at the Poleyard boat landing.

Fifty miles away from Myrtle Beach and two counties over.

Whoever abducted Brittanee knew exactly where they were going. The place was isolated, a rural country islet that only fishermen or locals would know about.

This was not the kind of place a seventeen-year-old girl would go to on Spring Break.

The investigators launched their search in the area that was about four miles in radius. Unfortunately, the terrain was treacherous. Alligators, wild hogs, snakes and biting insects the size of golf balls populated the area looking for their next meal.

Four-wheelers were brought in to keep the alligators away from the sniffing cadaver dogs. Investigators came to the site armed to shoot any wild hogs that came near.

"If her body is here," one investigator told Dawn in an ominous tone. "She would be eaten within six hours."

The search was frantic in the beginning but investigators seemed to lose hope after a few days passed. Britt's family returned home to Rochester with sunken hearts.

Brittanee's little brother chastized her friend upon their returning, stating "I thought you were bringing Brittanee back!"

Eight months later, police still had no promising leads. They would get an anonymous tip to check out an area a few miles north of the original search area near the Scantee River.

Once again, they came up with nothing. But a couple out fishing found a pair of sunglasses that looked as if they would belong to a teenage girl.

Neither her parents nor her boyfriend recognized the sunglasses as belonging to Brittanee. A DNA test was performed on the glasses and nothing was found.

Her mother continued to believe that she's alive.

"I think she was taken and held against her well," Dawn said. "I think she has become the victim of human trafficking."

Investigators and reporters shot down the notion, however. Typically, human trafficking occurs where the victim has a language barrier and Myrtle Beach was not exactly a hot bed for that type of crime. The police did not rule it out but it is low on their list of possibilities.

From 1997 to 2010, South Carolina has reported 12 cases of documented sex tracking. All were women, according to Doors to Freedom, an organization that helps victims of sex trafficking.

A few months later, police would receive some cell phone footage of Brittanee shot by a young man she had met. There were a group of teens antagonizing her and she wanted the young man's help to hang out with her so they would stop. He shot some footage of her sitting by herself, texting her boyfriend. He has since been cleared of any suspicion as he did have an alibi.

Pressed for suspects, law enforcement looked at every possible lead.

Three years later, authorities identified fifty-one year old Raymond Moody as a person of interest. They obtained a search warrant for a Georgetown motel room where Moody rented out at the time of Brittanee's disappearance. They noted that Moody had received a traffic ticket in Surfside beach just one day after Brittanee went missing.

Moody was a a registered sex offender, having raped a nine-year old girl in 1983. He was released in June of 2004. But Moody did not cooperate with investigators and remained tight-lipped under interrogation.

He is also a suspect in the case of Crystal Soles who disappeared in January of 2005.

"We've heard his name before," Dawn Drexel said. "It's a possibility the cases are connected. We don't know what happened to Crystal or Brittanee."

Moody lived in an area where Brittanee's cell phone last pinged. He was referred to as "Mr.Clean" because of his resemblance to the bald character in the Mr. Clean commercials. He has not been mentioned in any police reports since 2012, however.

The FBI would get involved and offer their belief that Brittanee was abducted and taken to a "stash house" where she was raped and then murdered. Her body was then wrapped in plastic and she was thrown into an alligator pit where her body would presumably be eaten.

This narrative was offered by FBI Agent Gerrick Munoz who obtained the informaton from an inmate named Taquan Brown. Brown is serving a 25-year sentence for a different case but stated he was present during Britt's last moments.

He said he had seen Britt when he visited a "stash house" which was a moniker used by drug dealers to describe a place where they stashed weapons, money or drugs.

Brown stated that Taylor picked Britt up in Myrtle Beach and took her to McClellanville. Once there he "showed her off, introduced her to some other friend that were there…they ended up tricking her out with some of their friends, offering her to them and getting a human trafficking situation."

The stash house was in the McClellanville area, the last location where Britt's cell phone was pinged.

Brown told the officials that he saw Da'Shaun Taylor, who was 16 years old at the time, and several other men "sexually abusing Brittanee Drexel."

Brown then claimed he went to the backyard to give Da'Shaun's father money.

During this time, Britt tried to escape. She was caught by one of the men who "pistol whipped" her across the head. She was then taken back inside the house.

Brown stated that he heard two gunshots and then saw the woman being wrapped up and removed from the home.

The FBI agent revealed that "several witnesses" have told him that she was dumped in a pond that was filled with alligators.

Taylor has since been convicted of robbery in 2011 and could face a life sentence. He stated that he knows nothing of Britt's case and with the lack of evidence he has not faced any charges in her disappearance.

Chad Drexel, however, thinks Taylor may have been involved.

He recalled a time when he was out handing out Brittanee's missing person fliers and handed it to Taylor who was in his car.

"I gave him the flier," Chad said. "He had a car full of brothers, friends. He handed the flier to one guy in the back seat. They all laughed and then drove away and threw the flier out the window."

"I got mad. I said 'There's something about this guy…'"

After the information was released to the public, Taylor's mother, Reverend Joanne Taylor, immediately defended her son.

She stated that he had already served his time for the robbery (a McDonald's restaurant) and that he was a "great kid" that was only

16 years old at the time of Brittanee's disappearance. During her son's hearing, Taylor's mother took the stand and said the following:

"And I want to say that at the time of this alleged abduction, he was 16 years old. I was never a mother thatwould let my kids run loosely, and definitely not with the father, you know, out to do things. I kept great hold on him. I am a pastor of a church. They were in church, they had a strict bedtime, I knew every place that they went. MyrtleBeach would not be a place that he would go at the age of 16. So I just, you know, I ask for your fairness, I ask for, you know, the correct justice in this case. And know that he is not a flight risk. I mean, I teached them good values, I instill in them what few things that have happened, they have exemplified overall what I've taught them. He is not, you know, a flight risk or anything.

Chad Drexel read the testimony and immediately took to his own Facebook page.

*I would like to set the record STRAIGHT with a STRONG REPLY to Joan Taylor's comments to the Post Courier in South Carolina this past Friday.*

*Based on evidence the FBI and the Myrtle Beach Police department has gathered, along with FACTS and SPECIFIC INFORMATION gathered from a team of Private Investigators that I HIRED to work with local law enforcement actively during the case (which will SOON COME TO LIGHT) – we have no doubt Timothy Da'Shaun Taylor played a significant role in the abduction and murder of my daughter.*

*Of course the mother of Timothy Da'Shaun Taylor is going to defend her son – as a father I can understand a need to defend your children. What I DON'T understand is defending your children when you must KNOW the truth.*

*Her assumptions and words stated have been verified INCORRECT and couldn't be farther from the TRUTH. We know Timothy Da'Shaun Taylor was witnessed by others (Witnesses NOT IN JAIL) with my daughter – we are just praying that they do the RIGHT thing and stop forward with what they know. Additionally he has been seen and followed to the EXACT area where my daughter's DNA was found. Joan Taylor claimed that the FBI and government are falsely accusing her son because of witnesses IN JAIL?! Well, we have other specific evidence, that I can NOT disclose at this time for the safety of my daughters case, which corroborates these testimonies!! Timothy Da'Shaun Taylor is KNOWN to be involved in dog fighting, bringing drugs to parties, and raping women (mostly Caucasian young women) he either picks up UNWILLINGLY or friends of friends that end up being drugged and taken there. This IS ONLY THE BEGINNING!! There is a TON more "EVIDENCE and HORRIBLE INFO" we would like the PUBLIC in that area be aware of for their safety, but we are unable to disclose at this time.*

*WITHOUT A DOUBT ..........Timothy Da'Shaun Taylor is a suspect in my daughter's Disappearance and Murder! My family and I will be following the FBI's requests to keep specific details in our daughter's case under wrap until THIS HORRIBLE PIECE OF TRASH goes to Prison for Life. After the guilty verdict, we will be happy to dispel these fairy tales that are being spun by Timothy's family. It is disgraceful the way this FAMILY and their FRIENDS are supporting and claiming innocence of a "PROVEN"*

*FELON without even looking at the evidence presented and the FACTS surrounding the case.*

*Also adding this PIECE OF TRASH photo so everyone can see WHO HE IS!*

On March 25th, 2017, FBI agents called Dawn Drexel to inform her they may have located Brittanee's remains. They are now searching an area 45 miles north of their previous search spot.

After two days, however, they gave up the search.

The case is ongoing.

# BEAUMONT CHILDREN

It was a warm summer morning on January 26, 1966, when the three Beaumont children left their suburban home to celebrate Australia Day at the beach. The children regularly made the trip by themselves, so their mother felt at ease providing them with bus fare and sending them on their way while she visited and had lunch with a close friend. However, she would return home that afternoon to find that the children still had not returned. That morning would end up being the last time she saw her three children.

Jane (aged 9), Arnna (aged 7), and Grant (aged 4), lived in Somerton Park, a quiet suburb minutes away from Adelaide, South Australia. Their father, Jim Beaumont, was a linen goods salesman who frequently traveled for work and their mother, Nancy Beaumont, was a stay-at-home mother.

The oldest child, Jane, was viewed by her parents as responsible enough to supervise the other children for short trips and adventures, a style of parenting that was the norm in Australia at that time. The children frequently took the five-minute bus ride to neighboring Glenely Beach by themselves and were looking forward to celebrating the national holiday at the beach.

The children left their home at 10:00am that morning and were seen arriving at the beach by witnesses at 10:15am. They spent much of that morning at play on the beach and were supposed to arrive home at 2:00pm. When they did not arrive at the appointed time, their mother assumed that they had become preoccupied with celebrating the holiday with their playmates and that they would arrive on the next bus or had decided to walk home, something that the three children had done before. When the children did not disembark from the next scheduled bus, their mother began to grow worried.

The disappearance of the Beaumont children would result in one of the largest manhunts and police investigations in Australian history.

Furthermore, the event had widespread consequences on Australian society, shattering the illusion that many parents had regarding their children's safety and changing the way that Australians parented their children forever.


Timeline of Events

10:00am - The children leave their Somerton Park home to travel to Glenely Beach by bus.

10:15am - They are seen exiting the bus by multiple witnesses.

11:00am - The three children are spotted playing beneath a sprinkler by an elderly woman. A tall blond man is spotted lying on the ground next to them, watching the children play.

11:15am - A tall blond man is seen playing with the children. They all appear to be laughing and at ease.

11:45am - The children purchase several pastries and a meat pie from the beach snack shop.

12:15pm - The tall blond man and the children are seen leaving the beach together. The children are witnessed laughing together and holding hands.

3:00pm - A postman on his route spots the children walking along Jetty Road alone, away from the beach. The postman is known to the children and they exchange greetings. Police believe that the timeline for this event is incorrect.

7:20pm - The parents of the children become gravely concerned and file a missing children's report with the local police department. Jim Beaumont and the local police search the entire Glenely Beach area.

8:40pm - Police search the surrounding beaches with no results. The father contacts friends and relatives in an attempt to locate the children.

10:00pm - Police issue public radio announcements with a missing children report.

Points of Interest

There are several details in this story which raised doubts with both the parents of the children and the local police department. When the children departed for Glenely Beach in the morning of January 26th, they left with only enough money to cover their bus fare: six shilling and a sixpence. However, the shop owner, who sold several pastries and a meat pie to the children at 11:45am, reported that the children paid for the food with a $1 bill, an amount of money that they did not have when they left their mother's care.

In addition, the shop owner knew the children well and had sold them food and pastries several times before. He reported that the children had never purchased a meat pie before. This suggests that the children received the money from someone after leaving their parents home and that they may have been purchasing the meat pie for someone else.

Lastly, the mother of the children, Nancy Beaumont, repeatedly said that her children were quite shy and very unlikely to speak with strangers, indicating that they may have met the tall blond man prior to the date of their disappearance. Their mother also remembered a seemingly innocuous comment from Arnna, who had previously told her mother that Jane had "got a boyfriend down the beach." Nancy assumed that her daughter was referring to a young playmate, but in hindsight it seems that she may have been referring to the tall blond man spotted by witnesses.

Police Investigation

The South Australian police force began investigating the disappearance of the children in full-force the evening of their disappearance. After interviewing several witnesses who were present at Glenely Beach, they were able to determine that the children were playing with a tall blond, "thin-faced" man while at the beach. He was described as being a blond man in his late 30s with a thin or athletic build.

"Things seemed bungled from the get-go," forensic psychologist Paula Orange said. "First off, the artist drawing the picture admitted to being drunk at the time of completing his task. So the sketch made of the suspect looks more like a lantern-jawed alien than a real person. Secondly, the witnesses claimed that the man was in his late thirties. Witnesses are notorious for getting ages wrong and the police dismissed too many possible subjects out of hand because they didn't fit the profile."

Several witnesses stated that the man was seen dressing the children prior to leaving the beach. The children's parents said that the kids, especially Jane, were very shy and unlikely to speak to a stranger. This later led police to theorize that the children had met the man in question prior to the date of their disappearance and had grown to know him over a period of several weeks.

The blond man and three children were seen leaving the beach together at 12:15pm, after the children purchased several pastries and a meat pie from a local vendor with a $1 bill, an amount of money that they did not have when they left their home that morning.

A wrench was thrown into the investigation when a postman, who knew the children and was on friendly terms with them, reported that he saw the children around 3:00pm that afternoon walking away from the beach and in the direction of their home in Somerton Park. He stated that he exchanged greetings with the young children and that they seemed to be in good spirits. In particular, the postman said that he say the children were "holding hands and laughing" as they walked down the road alone, with no blond companion in sight. Police later said that they believed the postman was mistaken about the timeline and that he most likely saw the children walking some time before noon.

Several months later, a woman in a nearby neighborhood contacted police and told them that she had seen a man with two girls and a young boy enter an abandoned house on her street. She also reported seeing the young boy walking away from the house before he was roughly grabbed by, and returned to the house with, the older man. She never saw the man or children again.

"The response from the public was overwhelming," Orange said. "People drove from miles away to aid in the search. They combed the beach and drained part of it all to no avail. They found nothing, not a trace."

The police were quickly able to eliminate drowning as the cause of the children's disappearance as a result of several witnesses saying that they saw the children leave the beach around 12:15pm. Furthermore, all of the children's belongings were missing, lending further support to the theory that they left the beach. After speaking with the parents, the police were able to identify seventeen different items that were carried by the children that day, providing a list of items that could be used to identify their remains or whereabouts. However, the police's continue efforts continued to prove fruitless.

The Psychic Circus

On November 8, 1966, nearly a year after the children's initial disappearance, an internationally-renowned psychic from the Netherlands, Gerard Croiset, was flown to Australia to investigate the case. His presence caused a whirlwind of media coverage in Australia and across the world. After making a series of outlandish and ever-changing claims, Croiset claimed that the children were buried underneath a warehouse just minutes away from the children's school.

"I appreciate him (Gerard Croiset) coming out to find the children," Jim Beaumont said. "But I don't believe what he said. I don't believe the children are dead and will continue to believe until given evidence that proves otherwise."

The building, which was under construction at the time of their disappearance, was eventually razed and excavated after the owners raised $40,000 for the project as a result of public pressure. No evidence of the children or their belongings were ever found.

"The press and police followed Croiset around everywhere," Orange said. "He was an obvious con artist but they were desperate. They had nothing."

A Series of Letters

Beginning in 1968, the parents of the three children began to receive a series of letters which rekindled hope in the idea that their children may still be alive. Postmarked from Dandernong, Victoria, the series of letters claimed to be written by Jane, the eldest daughter. She claimed to be under the supervision of a man and in good health and care, saying

Dear Mum and Dad,

We had a beautiful lunch today...The man is feeding us really well. The man took us to see The Sound of Music yesterday.

Police officers believed the letters to be from Jane after comparing them to examples of her handwriting and, as far as 1981, the Sidney Morning Herald produced analysis from handwriting experts claiming that the letters were actually from the missing child.

Following receipt of the letters supposedly sent from Jane, the parents received a letter from a man claiming to be in possession of the children. He said that he was willing to hand the children over to the parents at a specific time and location. The Beaumonts arrived at the appointed time and location with an undercover police officer but no one showed. They later received a letter from the same man claiming that he saw the undercover police officer arrive with the parents and that he would now keep the children, ending any hope of a peaceful exchange.

In 1992, following another investigation and remarkable achievements in fingerprint technology, authorities identified the author of the letters as a local man who was just a teenager at the time of the hoax. He reportedly wrote and mailed the letters as "a joke."

False Closure

Then, in November 2013, South Australian police received an anonymous tip claiming that the children were buried underneath a warehouse located in North Plympton. Although radar identified "one small anomaly, which can indicate movement or objects within the soil," no evidence was ever found.

The Suspects

Bevan Spencer von Einem

Bevan Spencer von Einem has long been considered the prime suspect in the disappearance of the Beaumont children. Einem was convicted of the July 1983 murder of fifteen-year-old Richard Kelvin, son of a popular news reporter, in 1984. Police have long suspected Einem of working with a series of accomplices and of having committed other abductions and murders.

In 1983, a police informant known as "Mr. B" told police that Einem claimed to have taken three children from a beach to perform medical "experiments," claiming that he performed "brilliant surgery" on the three children before accidentally killing one of them. Following the child's accidental death, the informant stated that Einem claimed to have killed the other two children and buried them in an open field outside the city of Adelaide.

Einem did bare some resemblance to the descriptions of the tall blond man given to police following the disappearance of the Beaumont children and was known to frequent Glenely Beach to spy on people in the changing rooms. He was also noted as having an obsession with children.

Einem worked as an accountant and lived with his mother. There were rumors that he was part of a ring of Adelaide professionals who shared a "hobby" of kidnapping, drugging and raping boys.

"Einem did match the description of the police sketches," Orange said. "And he did like to frequent the same beach. He seemed more interested in young teenage males as his list of known victims would indicate. Einem was a homosexual who picked up hitchhikers with his transvestite friend where they would engage in a "rough trade" style of sex. He would take photographs of his victims as a keepsake. The three young children would seem to be outside of his modus operandi."

However, Einem was significantly younger than the suspect described by witnesses; Einem was around 20 years old at the time, while the description of the suspect placed him in his late 20s. But, in 2007 local police officers identified a young man who looked exactly like a young Einem in Channel 7 news footage of the incident taken days after the disappearance. He remains a prime suspect in the case.

"The newly found news footage does implicate Einem in a psychological way," Orange said. "Killers often like to return to the scene of the crime. He was spotted on film, days after the disappearance. What are the odds against that?"

Arthur Stanley Brown

Arthur Stanley Brown, along with Einem, is considered to be one of two prime suspects in the abduction of the Beaumont children. In 1988, Brown, then 86 years old, was charged with kidnapping, raping, and murdering Judith and Susan Mackey in Townsville, Queensland. His first trial was declared a mistrial after the jury failed to reach a verdict in the case and his second trial was blocked because he was declared unfit to stand trial; Brown was suffering from dementia and Alzheimer's disease by this time.

He is considered one of two prime suspects in the case because of his connection to the murder of other children and because of his remarkable resemblance to descriptions of the tall blond man seen with the children at the time of their disappearance. He was also a prime suspect in the Adelaide Oval case, which involved the disappearance of Joanna Ratcliffe and Kirste Gordon.

"Brown was a known pedophile by his closest family members," Orange said. "He is alleged to have molested numerous younger relatives. He could be placed in the same area and time of the Beaumont children but nothing could be proven."

Although Brown is considered to be a prime suspect in the disappearance of the Beaumont children, the suspect in the case was identified as being in his late 30s; Brown was in his 50s at the time. Brown died in 2002 without ever admitting to the crime.

"Brown would move into a nursing home at the end of his life," Orange said. "He would die an innocent man with the courts never able to officially charge him because of his Alzheimer's."

James Ryan O'Neill

James Ryan O'Neill, convicted of murdering nine-year-old Ricky John Smith in the Australian state of Tasmania in 1975 and currently serving a life sentence for the crime, was considered as a suspect in the Beaumont children disappearance for some time. He is reported as having told several friends in the early 1970s that he was responsible for the disappearance of the Beaumont children in 1966. However, he was publicly eliminated as a suspect by the South Australian police. He remains in prison in Tasmania to this day.

"O'Neill was the subject of a documentary called 'The Fishermen,'" Orange said. "In the documentary, he is evasive about being the man behind the disappearance of the children. He is, however, at the forefront of most pundits who have studied the story. While Brown and Einem did not have charming personas, O'Neill did. He was handsome and smiley with the ability to manipulate everyone around him. He could fabricate lies at the drop of a hat so it is easy to believe that he would be able to charm the children into his acquaintance. People who knew him all described him as 'the most likable man you'll ever meet.' No one could believe that he would be capable of such an act."

Derek Ernest Percy

In 2007, the Victorian newspaper The Age published a report stating that Derek Ernest Percy, at the time the longest-serving prisoner in the southeastern Australian state, was responsible for the disappearance of the Beaumont children in 1966. Initially jailed in 1970 for the 1969 murder of 12-year-old Yvonne Tuohy, Percy was found not guilty of the crime by reason of insanity, but was nonetheless jailed "indefinitely."

He is widely considered to be Australia's worst child serial killer and is suspected of the killings of the Beaumont children, as well as the abduction, attempted rape, and stabbing of Marianne Schmidt and Christine Sharrock on January 11, 1965. In October 2014, Percy was also ruled to have abducted and killed seven-year-old Linda Stilwell in 1968. However, Percy passed away from cancer in 2013, having never admitted to any of his crimes. He remains a possible suspect in the case.

"Percy is unique in that he may have had his mother not aiding him but covering up for him," Orange said. "He is certainly one of the most sadistic pedophiles on record, his doings are unmentionable out of respect for his victims. He was in the city at the time of the Beaumont children disappearance and is probably the top suspect along with O'Neill. His mother, however, has thrown out a lot of what could have been evidence in the case."

Related Cases

Two similar cases to the disappearance of the Beaumont children attracted widespread attention in the South Australian media, and the primary suspect in the Beaumont children's kidnapping case was convicted in one case and suspected in the other.

The Adelaide Oval Case

On August 25, 1972, two young girls, Joanne Ratcliffe (aged 11) and Kirste Gordon (aged 4) went missing while attending an Australian football game. They are presumed dead. This case also received widespread attention in the South Australian media and

Bevan Spencer von Einem was considered the primary suspect in their disappearance.

Einem matched the descriptions of the tall blond man provided by witnesses in the Beaumont children's case and closely resembles the police sketch released to the public. A private police report in leaked in 1989 identified Einem as the primary suspect in the case.

The Family Murders

From 1973 to 1983, a group of men is believed to have been involved in the abduction, rape, and murder of a series of young men and male teenagers in the Adelaide area. Five teens were killed during this time period, including Alan Barnes (aged 16), Neil Muir (aged 25), Peter Stogneff (aged 14), Mark Langley (aged 18), and Richard Kelvin (aged 15). All victims were abducted and subjected to extended bouts of torture and physical assault, including sexual assault and medical experimentation.

Bevan Spencer von Einem was convicted of the abduction and murder of Richard Kelvin 1984 and is currently serving life in prison in Port Augusta prison. In 1990, he was also charged with the murder of Alan Barnes and Mark Langley, but key evidence from the Richard Kelvin murder was ruled inadmissible in the trial. Following the ruling against this key evidence, the prosecution dropped these charges against Einem on December 21, 1990.

Although Einem was the only member of this group to be convicted, and four out of five of The Family Murders remain unsolved, law enforcement officials believe that Einem was part of a white-collar group that preyed on young children. He remains the prime, and only living, suspect in the disappearance of the Beaumont children.

Impact on the Parents

Jim and Nancy Beaumont continued to hold out hope of finding their children for several decades after their disappearance. In fact, the couple continued to live at the Somerton Park home, at 109 Harding Street, that they shared with their children for nearly two decades, hoping that the children would return home someday. Nancy Beaumont was reported as saying that it would be "dreadful" if the children returned to the home only to find that their parents had moved.

"The Beaumonts left the rooms of the children untouched," Orange said. "Every toy, every book even the bed was left exactly as the children had left them."

The couple were never considered as suspects in the case and cooperated with the police at every turn in the investigation, including working with the police and searching in vain every time a new lead developed in the case over the next several decades.

According to The Age, the parents "have since separated, but still live in Adelaide." The stress and sorrow that resulted from their children's abduction, combined with the constant new leads and media attention is said to have contributed to the failure of their marriage.

Jim, in particular, is said to still be suffering from intense and inconsolable grief every time a new development is reported. Nancy was also reported to have suffered extreme grief and horror when, in 1990, several Australian newspapers released computer-generated images of what her children would look like after aging several decades. She reportedly refused to look at the pictures.

"Jim was a little bit stronger than Nancy," Orange said. "He would address the media more than she did. But they both suffered terribly for the rest of their lives into their eighties. They would spend over fifty years wishing for their children's return, getting false hope after false hope, one false lead after another which would all ultimately turn up nothing. It was a horrific cruelty."

Lastly, Jim and Nancy have largely been seen as sympathetic and pitiable figures in the Australian media and in society at large. Although their actions may seem reckless or irresponsible by today's standards, Australian society was viewed as extremely safe in the 1960s and their policy of allowing a child to supervise their younger siblings both in the home and in public was practiced by a large portion of Australian parents.

Impact on Australian Society

The disappearance of the Beaumont children became an overnight sensation in Australia, led to one of the largest police searches in the country's history, and remains the most famous missing persons case in the country. Prior to this incident, Australia was largely viewed as one of the safest societies on the planet and children were allowed to roam freely, doors remained unlocked at all times, and there was little fear of strangers. All of that changed overnight.

"Australia lost its innocence with the disappearance of the Beaumont Children," Orange said. "For three young children to disappear was unheard of. The city where they grew up was a dignified place, a safe place. But it was all an illusion that went away the day the children went missing."

During the initial search for the children, Jim Beaumont went on national television to appeal for their safe return. His heartfelt address to the nation had a lasting impact on the parents and children who watched his plea. Hundreds of viewers called into the station to offer tips and Australian police report that hundreds of tips continue to come in every year to this day. His image on national television continues to serve as a warning for those who believe in the incorruptibility of their fellow citizens and in the safety of their country.

"A lot of people today will blame the parents for letting them go on the bus alone," Adelaide resident Rachel Harding said. "But times were different back then. Back then kids would walk to school by themselves. Kids were told not to talk to strangers. The Beaumonts did tell their children to not talk to children. But child molesters are cunning monsters. My guess is that he may have stolen the eldest child's purse then conned them into seeing him as their benefactor. They would not have had money to get home then along comes this "blonde man" who offers them money. Buys them food and promises to take them home."

Children who came of age in Australia during the 1960s have remarked that there was a definite culture shift following the Beaumont children's disappearance, often describing a "before" and "after." While children were once allowed to roam freely and interact with strangers, Australian parents have since altered their style of parenting and curtailed the amount of freedom offered to young children.

"It was the type of case where we believe there was a lone offender," Australian police detective Des Bray said. "It isn't the type of crime where one would go around bragging about. But we do hope that he told someone and that somebody knows something."

If the Beaumont children are alive today, they would all be in their 50s and would have lived through years of hearing their names and story broadcast on national television and reported on breathlessly in national newspapers. Despite the vast amount of information we have on the case, their fates may never be known with any certainty.

Both Jim and Nancy Beaumont are still alive, and as of this writing they are ninety and eighty-years old respectively. The anonymous tips and false hopes continue to come in today as they did over fifty years ago.

# THE STRANGE DISAPPEARANCE OF PATRICIA MEEHAN

70

NATHAN NIXON

## Patricia Meehan Disappearance

The story of Patricia Meehan is a very strange and puzzling one. She seemingly disappeared into the night with little reason. The case has remained unsolved since 1989. With few witnesses, the full events are sketchy at best. What is well known about this case is that our culture has seemingly thought of every possible scenario to explain what happened to her. To understand and possibly solve the case, understanding the person that Patricia Meehan was is of paramount importance.

Patricia Meehan was never afraid of change. Her path of life took her all over the United States and to nearly every type of region. She was born on November 1, 1951 in Pittsburgh, Pennsylvania. She lived a typical life. She was said to have been "the perfect child" by her loving parents and by all who knew her. She had great ambition to see the world and to attack life with a smile. Socially she was on the same level as her peers. When she decided to attend college in Oklahoma City, Oklahoma, no one was really surprised. That was who Patricia was. That is exactly what she did.

She studied early childhood development and earned her degree in four years of college study. Again, she was living the American dream and successfully setting up a future to thrive. She made many friends in Oklahoma, even though it was a foreign place to a young woman from Pittsburgh. She took up a career in early childhood caregiving in Oklahoma and thrived in the profession for nearly 10 years. She was unhappy, or perhaps, unfulfilled in her work. She sporadically spoke with her family and a few friends from back home in Pennsylvania at the time. People knew Patricia to take risks. She was never afraid to change her outlook if it meant a new adventure or perhaps a new challenge lay ahead. In 1985, she made a major life change that would, effectively, lead to her ultimate disappearance.

She had informed her parents in the years prior that she wanted to become involved in animal care. She made this a reality when she moved to Bozeman, Montana in 1985. She moved alone. Patricia was not married and had left her simple, safe life behind in Oklahoma to pursue a career as a ranch hand. While this major career shift was motivated to start a happier life, it ultimately didn't always pay the bills. She worked numerous odd-jobs in the industry and could successfully make ends meet on her own. She continued this new lifestyle for four years in Bozeman, Montana.

The last person that can be fully confirmed to have seen Patricia Meehan alive was her landlord. Meehan's landlord reported to police investigators later that she seemed much more hyper than normal. This struck the landlord as extremely odd for the normally mellow, collected Patricia. Nonetheless, there were absolutely no problems between the two in any way. Patricia always paid her rent and was an "overall great tenant" to have.

The evening of April 20, 1989 is one of great speculation as to what really happened. The testimony of Peggy Bueller has always been a key component to the theories of Patricia's disappearance.

At approximately 8:05 P.M. Peggy Bueller and her father were traveling west bound on Montana State Highway 200. They were passing through the tiny town of Circle, Montana. To their surprise, they could see a set of vehicle headlights heading straight at them up ahead. A vehicle heading east was driving on the wrong side of the road. Peggy managed to swerve onto the shoulder and avoid a head-on collision with the opposing driver. The car that had been following behind Peggy was driven by an off-duty police dispatcher named Carol Heitz. Unfortunately for Carol, she was not able to swerve and avoid a collision.

Peggy Bueller had pulled over and gazed in her rear-view mirror in time to see the collision with the car driven by Carol Heitz. Thankfully, no injuries occurred in the accident. The story is very odd and somewhat eerie from this point. Just after impact, Carol Heitz emerged from her vehicle unharmed. She was shook up, but suffered no major injury. Being a police dispatcher, her first concern was for the other driver. The car that was traveling east bound was driven by Patricia Meehan. Patricia was next to emerge from her car after the impact. She stood in the middle of the road, and proceeded to slowly approach the car of Carol Heitz. According to Heitz, Patricia Meehan did not utter a single word. "She approached me calmly and silently," Heitz reported. "She seemingly stared directly through me from the moment she began to approach me."

Peggy Bueller remained in her vehicle and observed what was taking place. What she observed was "one of the strangest acts" she had ever seen. Peggy and Heitz agree that Patricia climbed over a fence just off of the road after she passed by Carol. She took only a step after getting over the fence and turned back around to stare upon the accident. She made no noise or any sort of expression. She stood there for at least two minutes. Heitz described Meehan as someone who seemed to be observing the accident scene rather than someone who had been involved in the accident. After a few short minutes, Meehan turned around and walked into a secluded Montana field into the pitch dark night. This was the last confirmed sighting of Patricia Meehan. By the time police arrived to sort out the accident, the whereabouts of Patricia were unknown. Peggy and Carol gave the exact same story in separate interviews with investigators. As eerie as the accident had unfolded, it had ended quietly and abruptly. Patricia Meehan was officially gone.

Peggy Bueller quickly drove into town when Patricia disappeared into the night. Her father stayed with Carol Heitz at the scene of the accident. Peggy reached a phone within ten minutes and alerted the authorities. When police arrived, an extensive search of the field where Patricia was seen walking away to turned up nothing. It only took police 15 minutes to identify the then mystery woman as Patricia Meehan after they ran the license plate of the vehicle. She was a registered member of the Bozeman, Montana community and had no criminal record. This was shocking to police who had assumed the woman left due to the fact that police would be arriving to the scene to investigate the accident. This posed the burning question that is still unanswered of why this woman would leave the scene of the accident if she had no criminal record.

Police made efforts to investigate the field immediately following the accident. Police discovered a tennis shoe about a mile into the field that had been accompanying a trail of footprints. The shoe matched what would have been the approximate size of the foot of Patricia Meehan. Oddly enough, the tracks seemingly disappear. Due to darkness, the investigation was suspended until the following morning of April 21. When police arrived to further check for a trail, the footprints led to nothing. The terrain had an influence in this as well as the fact that the actual shoe prints were gone, likely due to Patricia going barefoot at this point in her walk. Police had no leads.

There were two major theories that investigators had arrived at to this point. The first was the most likely. They believed that Patricia had hitchhiked from a small rural road in the area with a trucker. This could obviously not be confirmed, however the lack of a body, further clothes or footprints, as well as a lack of any whereabouts in surrounding cities points to this to be the likely case. The second theory they had suggest that she stowed away in a hay truck in the area and accomplished the same thing. This proved later to be unlikely as no hay trucks were confirmed to be in the field or in the immediate area.

The Meehan family arrived to Montana from Pittsburgh in the day following the accident. They distributed over 2,000 missing person flyers in the surrounding Montana towns and provided police with valuable information. The flyers turned up numerous calls, however none of these would lead to finding Patricia. Over 500 local volunteers searched the mountainous terrain around the accident site in an effort to possibly locate Patricia. For days, people walked the area. Some even brought dogs to perhaps catch a scent trail. These searches turned up absolutely nothing. There was no evidence of human activity in the mountains, and there were no evidence of a body or struggle in the surrounding area. Patricia had seemingly disappeared without a trace after taking a path into a secluded field. Perhaps the events in the days and weeks prior could shed some light into who Patricia was and things she had been recently going through.

The Meehan family revealed to police that Patricia had been going through some dark times in the past couple of months. Patricia was somewhat at a dead end and was feeling lost. She had asked her parents if she could return home in an effort to get back on track. Her parent's agreed, but only if she see a psychologist leading to coming home. Patricia agreed. She was diagnosed as suffering from depression. Ironically, she had an appointment with her psychologist the morning after the accident on April 21. She obviously never made this appointment.

Police also were suspicious as to why Patricia was even in this part of the state anyway. She had an appointment in Bozeman, Montana for the next morning. Bozeman was where she was living. The direction of travel she was taking at the time of the accident was in the opposite direction of Bozeman. Investigators asked the Meehan family if they had any idea where she may be going or what she was doing in this remote part of Montana. They had absolutely no idea. It was evident to police that she had no intention of returning to Bozeman to make her appointment the next morning. But could there be more to this part of the story?

The Meehan family had a roll of film developed that had been found in Patricia's car the night of the accident. The film was fully used. There were numerous pictures of nature. Beautiful countryside and the secluded area that Patricia loved. There were also numerous pictures of animals, specifically horses, that Patricia had devoted her life to in the recent years. Patricia's family stumbled across one picture that was quite alarming. A random picture that Patricia had taken in front of a mirror.

She had a very confused look on her face and seemed lost. Investigation of the picture by mental professionals led some to believe she could have been suffering from amnesia. This could obviously not be proven, but would go further in explaining the odd behavior she displayed that night. Some of the investigators pointed to this as a possible reason that she was driving away from Bozeman and was 300 miles away from home. Could she simply have forgotten how to get home? Could her mental health had gotten that bad?

Patricia had been driving on the wrong side of the road and made no effort to swerve. Police drew two possible conclusions to this fact. The first was that she was so far lost in amnesia that she simply didn't think she was doing anything wrong or perhaps forgot the basic rules of driving. The second was that she was possibly trying to harm herself or had gotten so careless that the results were not clearly thought through. These are obviously speculation and will never be proven one way or the other. The mental health of Patricia was most assuredly in a low place.

The roll of film that was developed also proved something else to investigators and the Meehan family. Socially, she was in a dark place also. Out of every picture that had been developed, not one of them featured people that weren't named Patricia Meehan. This is clearly not the norm. Patricia had mentioned that she had had a few boyfriends since arriving in Montana, but nothing serious and committal. She had previously mentioned to her parents that she had become lonely and never really made any friends in her new home. This could help to explain the depression and possible mental health issues that she had developed.

Over the last 25 years, there have been over 5,000 reported sightings of Patricia Meehan. Through all of this, only 3 of those do police feel could be Patricia or are even likely to be her. In the days following her disappearance, there were some interesting leads that were generated by the public calls on the missing person flyers.

On May 4, 1989 just two weeks after the accident, a strong lead was generated out of Luverne, Minnesota. Out of all of the possible sightings, this is considered by police and those surrounding the case to be the most likely sighting of Patricia. A police officer in Luverne claimed to have seen Patricia sitting in a Hardee's restaurant by herself. For over five hours, she was sitting in corner booth drinking water. She remained until closing time, and then proceeded to walk to a nearby 24 hour diner. Here, the officer questioned her. The woman refused adamantly to give her name. She first said that she was from Colorado, and later said she was from Israel. The major problem with all of this is that the officer could not detain her. She had done nothing wrong. However, he left without further checking to identify her. This was perhaps the best chance to obtain Patricia if this indeed was her. The officer left and where this mystery woman went next is unknown.

Another interesting sighting occurred on May 19, 1989. This is nearly one full month after the accident. A waitress at a local restaurant in Bozeman, Montana reported seeing Patricia eating there. She informed police that Patricia at in a hurry and said she had to go shopping at 9 A.M. She said she was polite, but did seem to be displaying odd behavior. Another waitress on the same shift also reported seeing her. This waitress said she was talking to herself and seemed disoriented. Patricia left the restaurant and again, no attempts were really made to investigate who she really was.

The theories that surround this case are perhaps the most interesting in the current media. If Patricia was alive today, she would be in her late 60's. This would obviously make her hard to identify in the general public. This leads to the first theory.

The first, and generally most believed theory, is that Patricia simply wanted another fresh start. She had done this in the past, albeit in a much less drastic way. She wanted a fresh start after high school, so she attended college in Oklahoma City, Oklahoma. She wanted a career change and a change of passion nearly 10 years after she started her career, so she moved to Bozeman, Montana and became a ranch hand. Many feel that she again wanted a career change and a life change at this point in her life. Turning to her parents, they gave her an ultimatum to see a psychologist before she came home. The theory suggest that she wasn't happy with her family about this. She obtained her fresh start by planning an event that would allow her to vanish into the unknown. What better place to accomplish this than a secluded highway in rural Montana where she could simply walk away.

This theory goes on further to explain that she had walked across the field and met up with someone who would drive her away. This theory doesn't sound too crazy at this juncture. The who or why is unknown, but the basis of the theory is mostly sound. Where she would have started this new life is completely unknown. But for a person who was struggling socially, not completely happy, and perhaps not enjoying the rural life as much as she had anticipated, this theory makes some sense.

The second popular theory is the more logical, medically supported theory. The collision that Patricia Meehan had was significant. While there were no injuries on the exterior, a concussion is without a doubt a possibility of this type of vehicle accident. Some believe that it was not amnesia to blame, but a concussion that would cause her to act so disoriented after the accident. The theory suggest that she exited her vehicle with a head injury and collapsed in the field shortly after beginning her walk into the night.

Montana is home to vast amounts of wildlife and has a very abstract climate. The night time temperatures in April in Montana typically are going to approach freezing. Anything under 50 degrees at altitude is going to be a severe situation for a minimally clothed, small woman with a possible head injury. The theory suggest that she was unconscious overnight and perhaps was eaten by animals, which would explain the lack of a body or any other evidence to her disappearance. It is for this reason that the theory is typically not accepted. Even with this, there would have been signs of this happening by one of the numerous volunteers or investigators in the following days.

The disappearance of Patricia Meehan has garnered national attention for the past 25 years. On November 1, 1989 the case was featured on *Unsolved Mysteries.* This would have marked the 38th birthday for Patricia.

Sightings are still reported on Patricia and a host of other in the United States. With each passing year, it is all too assuring that this case will never be solved. The lack of information on the case is puzzling. Those who choose to research the case will find that there is little information beyond the night of the accident and some significant reported sightings. All of these factors have led to a disappearance that has stumped police since that fateful night.

Patricia Meehan was an ambitious woman. She took risk in efforts to accomplish her goals and to get the most out of life. Anyone who ever knew her would say that she was a wonderful person with a positive view of the world. She loved her family dearly, and she loved her life deeply. She confidently left home to discover new opportunities on multiple occasions. It seems that life perhaps got too much for her in Montana. Maybe she just wanted to come home. Whatever the case, Patricia Meehan disappeared in April 1989, and has yet to be found. This beautiful young woman hasn't officially turned up in over 25 years. This tragic case may never be closed. A sure fact of the case is that Patricia was a sweet woman who didn't get in this situation by means of risky behavior or negative interactions. Likely, her disappearance can be attributed to a social low spot where she needed help that she didn't go through with getting. Maybe one day the truth of where her walk ultimately led will come out.

## FOR MORE TRUE CRIME CLICK HERE[1]

---

1. http://www.pochepictures.com/truecrime.html

bonus:

Arlis Kay Perry was a newly married nineteen-year-old when she entered Stanford Memorial Church at Stanford University in the late night hours of October 12th, 1974. She would be found the next morning, the victim of a brutal murder in what appeared to be a ritualistic killing.

Her case has remained unsolved for the past forty-two years. Various rumors and theories abound as to who her murderer was. There is conjecture that she was the victim of the Son of Sam, the Zodiac Killer, the Death Angels and the Process Church.

The police never obtained solid leads on her case and it remains as much a mystery today as it was over forty years ago.

Who killed Arlis Perry?

EARLY LIFE

Arlis was born on February 22nd, 1955 in Linton, North Dakota to Marvin Dykema and Jean Van Beek. She usually wore glasses and had her hair straight. In the lone picture of her available online, her hair is wavy and she is not wearing glasses. This is an unfamiliar look for her and no one knows where or when the picture was taken. She was small, at 5'6" and weighing 110 lbs.

Arlis would graduate from Bismarck High School in 1973 where she was a cheerleader and a member of the Fellowship of Christian Athletes. She had a high school sweetheart, Bruce Perry, and they were both born again Christians. Bruce would be accepted into Stanford University upon graduation while Arlis would stay behind in Bismarck. She remained active in her church as a Sunday school teacher in the Bismarck reformed church.

Then she came into contact with people from the Process Church.

They were six young men that were renting a home across the street from her grandmother. Their names were Father Christian, Brother Thomas, Brother Joseph and three other men who were called "initiates."

The men tried to initiate Arlis into their religion but she soon became disenchanted with their belief system.

She realized that the were devil worshipers.

Arlis then made it a point to try and proselytize anyone who was involved in their church, leading them from Satanism into Christianity.

THE PROCESS CHURCH

The Process Cult became controversial in the early 1970s with its strong ties to the Manson family. Their belief system allowed them to worship both Christ and Satan. The church started in both Los Angeles and New York but branched out to North Dakota, as its leaders wanted the isolation of the hills and woods.

They would have meetings at the Hillside Cemetery in Bismarck and a wooded area behind Mary College. It was here that they would steal the dogs of people who lived in a nearby trailer park and sacrifice them in satanic rituals. People were complaining that they would find their dogs lying dead inside a "majick circle", their bodies badly mutilated.

MOVING TO CALIFORNIA

After graduation, Arlis would continue to participate in the Fellowship of Christian Athletes as a "huddle leader" as well as taking a job as a receptionist in a dental office. She would attend the local junior college for a year as she corresponded with Bruce Perry who was in his first year of studies at Stanford.

Bruce would return home and ask for Arlis' hand in marriage. She would accept and join him as he returned for his second year in Stanford's pre-med program.

Bruce's studies did not leave a lot of time for Arlis and she became a bit restless. She would take a job as a receptionist at a law firm to occupy her time during the day when Bruce would be away, finding work at the law firm Spaeth, Blase, Valentine, and Klein in Palo Alto.

The couple lived at the Quillen House in Escondido Village which was a campus housing unit for married couples.

Arlis got into the habit of taking nightly walks around the campus. Bruce worried for her safety and advised her not to. She stopped the practice until one night she wanted to get out of the home and mail off some letters.

DEADLY CHURCH VISIT

On October 12th, 1974 at around 11: 30 pm, Bruce and Arlis were walking on the Stanford campus. They would discover that the tire on Arlis' car had gone flat. They would have a minor argument as to who was going to take care of it. Bruce went back to the dorm and Arlis would go to the Memorial Church, telling Bruce that she wanted to pray alone.

Arlis entered and several people remembered seeing her. A security guard told her that it was almost midnight and the church was about the close up. She remained inside, however, and witnesses remembered seeing a "sandy-haired man" walk inside.

Arlis didn't return home after several hours and Bruce went out to look for her.

When he didn't find her, he called the police.

The next morning at around 05:45 am, security guard Steve Crawford would discover her body inside the church.

In Maury Terry's book, "Ultimate Evil", he described Perry's murder scene as follows:

"She was found lying on her back, with her body partially under the first pew on the left side of the alcove, a short distance from where she had been seen praying. Above her was a large carving which had been sculptured into the church wall years before. It was an engraving of the cross. The symbolism was explicit.

Arlis's head was facing forward, toward the main altar. Her legs were spread wide apart, and she was nude from the waist down. The legs of her blue jeans were placed upside down across her calves, purposely arranged in that manner. Viewed from above, the resulting pattern of Arlis's legs and the inverted blue jeans took on a diamond-like shape.

Arlis's blouse was torn open, and her arms were folded across her chest. Placed neatly between her breasts was an altar candle. Completing the desecration, another candle, thirty inches long, was jammed into her vagina. She had been beaten and choked. Death was due to her an ice pick being rammed into her skull behind her left ear, the handle protruding grotesquely from her head."

THE AFTERMATH

Security guard Crawford stated that he had locked up the church a little after midnight. He rechecked that the doors were still locked at around 02:00 a.m.

At 03:00 a.m. Perry had called the police and informed them that his wife was missing. The Santa Clara County Sheriff's went to the church and found all of the doors locked. Crawford would return to the church at 05:45 to unlock the doors and he found the west side door open.

The obvious suspect was Bruce Perry and police immediately went to brutally interrogate him.

"You knew your wife was having an affair so you killed her!"

Perry adamantly denied the questions. The police gave him a polygraph test which he passed.

Investigators would found two pieces of identifying evidence from the scene. They were able to collect a DNA sample which was found in semen near the body. The second was a bloody palm print found on one of the candles.

"It's a typical-if there is such a thing-sexual psychopathic slaying," Santa Clara County Undersheriff Tom Rosa said.

Rumors began to circulate around the campus. Some people were saying that Arlis was the victim of a satanist torture rite called the "Black Mass."

Rosa disputed the claim.

"It has no cult-like overtones," Rosa said. "It just happened to occur in a church."

There were no signs of a struggle. The detectives believed that Arlis was the victim of a "fast and sudden attack" as she entered the church around midnight.

Bruce would tell authorities that she often went there to pray when she was having problems.

SON OF SAM

Conspiracy theories would abound as the murder would go unsolved for many years. Some believe that Arlis was not murdered by a lone psychopath but by a satanic cult who stalked her from Bismarck, North Dakota.

Because of the way Arlis' body was positioned (legs spread with a candlestick in her breasts and vagina) people familiar with occult activity assumed that this was a ritualistic killing.

Fueling the speculation was some cryptic correspondence from David Berkowitz.

Berkowitz, the "Son of Sam" killer from New York City, had mentioned the Perry killing as he wrote authorities in North Dakota. He said that he had information on the killer, a man he referred to as "Manson II."

In 1979, five years after the murder, Berkowitz would send police authorities in North Dakota a book. In the margin, he had written: "Arlis Perry, hunted, stalked and slain, followed to California, Stanford Univ."

Berkowitz would claim that he was not the only person involved in the string of New York murders, hinting that he was part of a larger Satanic cult.

Detectives would later interview Berkowitz regarding Perry's murder but realized that he had "nothing of value to offer."

Those following the case, however, believe that Berkowitz should have been interrogated harder.

"Why would he make it up? He had no motive, no reason," crime writer Maury Terry asked. "He's confessed to three murders, he's not getting out."

The "Manson II" Berkowitz referred to was William Mentzer. Mentzer was suspected of being the head of the Son of Sam cult, had ties to the Manson family (although not to Charles Manson himself) and was suspected of being the Zodiac killer.

But was he responsible for killing Arlis Perry?

The answer may lie in the fact that at some point Mentzer was involved in a "hit squad" involving the Process Church. He allegedly performed assassin duties for the higher-ups who needed someone killed.

Interestingly, the serial murders of the Zodiac Killer stopped after Mentzer was in prison There were numerous parallels between the Zodiac Killer and Mentzer. Detectives believe that the Zodiac had military training. Mentzer had served in the Marines during Vietnam and killed ten people. Upon his return from the Vietnam War, the killings began in December of 1968.

The Zodiac would stab two of his victims with a bayonet style knife with rivets. Mentzer had a job where he was making rivets at a local aerospace company.

The Zodiac killer than began taunting the newspapers, sending them a diagram of a bomb while threatening to blow up a school bus. Mentzer later had a job driving a bus. He also had military training in demolition and plastic explosives. One of the survivors said that the killer spoke in a slow monotone with a drawl. Mentzer speaks the same way.

After a final letter to the press, the Zodiac mysteriously vanished in 1974.

Menzer would later be arrested for his role in the brutal murders of Roy Radin in 1983 and a prostitute/madam named June Mincher in 1984.

Radin had been shot more than twenty times in the head. Menzer would then put a stick of dynamite in Radin's mouth and blow off his face.

In the end, however, police didn't believe Menzer had probable cause to be the Zodiac killer and he would never be questioned for the death of Arlis Perry despite the rumors.

Crime writer Terry would investigate Perry's murder on his own and retrace her steps. He thinks that as many as four people were responsible for her death. He believes that the "sandy-haired" man who visited Perry at the law firm was a cult member from Bismarck, someone that she knew from the Process Church.

"She (Arlis) might have heard or seen something she shouldn't have," he said. "They may have feared she would expose them. Someone in Bismarck OK'd this, and someone had the hooks to get help on the West Coast," he said. "This was a pretty sophisticated operation."

BRUCE PERRY

Bruce Perry would complete go on to become a researcher in children's mental health and the neurosciences, becoming an internationally recognized authority in his field.

At Arlis's funeral, one of her law firm co-workers was confused when he saw Bruce. He thought her husband was a different man who had come into the workplace earlier. He witnessed her get into a "heated argument" with the man and assumed it was her husband. The co-worker described this man as "sandy-haired' which would fit the description of the man seen following Arlis into the church the night she was murdered.

Arlis would also note that there were two Bruce Perrys listed in the phone book. There is some speculation that Mentzer pretended to be Bruce Perry and had his name listed in the phone book. People from North Dakota would call and get him instead of Arlis' husband. He would then be able to finagle her whereabouts but subtly asking the family member the right questions.

This is one of the more far-fetched theories. It doesn't seem plausible that Menzer would go to the lengths of putting out a fake name and phone number just to coax Arlis' family and friends to call. Furthermore, he was a black-haired, mustachioed man who did not fit the "sandy-haired" man description.

But what is curious is that Perry's killing would be another instance of a series of unsolved murders that took place in and around the Stanford campus in the early 1970s.

A SERIAL KILLER AT WORK?

The murder of Arlis would be the fourth homicide on the Stanford campus in less than two years as well as the third incident in which the victim was a young woman out alone.

None of the murders were ever solved.

The killings started with Leslie Marie Perlov, a 21-year old Stanford history graduate who worked as a Palo Alto law librarian. She was found strangled to death on February 16th, 1973 in the foothills behind the campus. She had disappeared after leaving her workplace three days earlier.

Perlov's body would be found in a wooded gully where she had a scarf that was "wrapped tightly around her throat." There was no sign of a struggle where her body was found leading authorities to believe she walked there on her own volition.

She was not sexually assaulted but her skirt had been pulled up around her waist and her pantyhose had been stuffed into her mouth. While officers were searching for Perlov, they would find the body of Mark Rosvold, a twenty-five-year-old man out of Palo Alto. Rosvold was believed to have committed suicide the morning after Perlov was murdered. Perlov was last seen near the quarry gate of the Stanford campus, talking to a man with long blonde hair.

Seven months after the Perlov murder, physics student David S. Levine would be found stabbed to death on a walkway just east of the Meyer Undergraduate Library. The attack was estimated to have occurred between 1 and 3 a.m.

An early morning jogger would find the body of Levine. The young man had been stabbed fifteen times in the back and the side.

Like the rest of the murders, there had been no sign of struggle. The detectives believed that the young man was taken by surprise. Levine's empty wallet remained in his pants pocket and they ruled out robbery as a motive for the murder.

Levine was a straight-A student and called brilliant by his fellow students.

San Francisco Mayor Joseph Alioto believed that the murders were the work of a cult called the "Death Angels" who were suspects in the "Zebra" killings in San Francisco. Three months after the murder of Levine, a slaying took place on the UC Berkeley campus that was also rumored to be the work of the "Death Angels."

The Death Angels were a genocidal Black Muslim faction who mostly killed white people from October 1973 to April 1974. They were compromised of four black men: Manuel Moore, Larry Green, Jessie Lee Cooks, J.C.X Simon. The group committed at least 15 murders according to Wikipedia. Author Clark Howard estimates the group to be responsible for as many as two-hundred seventy deaths.

The Death Angeles would use .32 caliber pistols to shoot their victims point blank, however. They would take people by surprise but there were not any instances where they used strangulation or a knife for the initial attack as was the case for Perlov and Levin.

On March 24th, 1974, Janet Ann Taylor was strangled while hitchhiking to her La Honda home after visiting a friend on the Stanford campus. Her body was found early the next morning in a roadside ditch. Taylor was twenty-one years old and the daughter of former Stanford athletic director, Chuck Taylor.

Detectives would later concede that there were "similarities" between the Perlov and Taylor murders.

Both would be strangled although Taylor would be choked by hand instead of a scarf. Neither were sexually violated.

Both were barefoot when their bodies were found and wearing raincoats. Neither of the purses were on the person when their bodies were found.

"We really don't know who we're looking for," Sheriff's Inspector Rudy Siemssen said after the Taylor killing. "We have no motive. She apparently had no money in her purse, although you could speculate that robbery was a motive. It's a rough one."

WHO KILLED THEM?

None of the unsolved Stanford murders seem to be connected in terms of the method of killing. But, on the surface, they all were senseless and without motivation.

In the case of Arlis, there is mere speculation because of her conversations with the Bismarck Process Cult. The rumor is that someone from the cult, a leader or ordered assassin, came out to California because she tried to convert their members to Christ.

What is curious about the case is how the body was positioned. Arlis' pants were moved but placed on top of her body. The pants were positioned legs up, across her calves and her legs were spread apart. Her arms were in a crucifix position and the altar candle was shoved in her vagina.

Looking at her body from above, she was positioned in the Mason's symbol of Freemasonry. So this suggests that her murder was the work of someone involved in the Freemason cult or someone who was trying to make it look as if there was Freemason involvement.

It also appeared that Arlis may have known her killer. Her meeting with the "sandy-haired" man at work or the church may have been a scheduled meeting place. She was a devout Christian woman, used to doing the right thing, so it seems a bit odd that she wouldn't obey the security guard when he told her he was closing up the church.

The speculation is that she was meeting someone, probably the "sandy-haired" man. Who he was or how they came to meet is the question of the day. The problem is that the police failed to see the cult link in the killing, with some kind of warped religious undertones. How much of an evangelist was Arlis and who exactly did she speak with at the Process Cult in Bismarck?

The police were never interested in pursuing that line of thought.

There were rumors in Bismarck that well-known people were part of a satanic cult that performed all kinds of grisly rituals at Pioneer Park and the caves behind the University of Mary. One witness reported that they remembered seeing people come into town in priest's outfits. Only they weren't wearing white collars. They were wearing red collars and upside-down cross necklaces.

Jon Martinson, a former psychology professor at Bismarck State College, doesn't buy the theory that Arlis was stalked from Bismarck to California.

"I remember a lot of weird religious stories going on around here in that time," Martinson said. "Like covens dancing under the full moon and rituals taking place down by the river bottoms. But in her case, I think she was at the wrong place at the wrong time."

After Terry's book "The Ultimate Evil" came out, students around the Bismarck around began trolling around the University of Mary looking for any semblance of satanic cult activity. They found none but it became an urban legend around the town. The caves behind the University of Mary were eventually filled in.

Terry still firmly believes that Berkowitz knew something that the police didn't follow-up on. "It's very important to know that it was Berkowitz himself who raised the connection to (the University of) Mary, and he did it in late 1979 – nearly eight years before The Ultimate Evil was published," Terry said. "Nothing about the Mary

(University of Mary) ties to Arlis' death was made public until the book came out. But Berkowitz knew about cult activities there all along. And I also confirmed that rituals had been occurring there in the 1970s."

Ken Kahn was one of the detectives who flew into Attica State Prison in New York to interview Berkowitz. The Son of Sam killer remained vague and didn't fess up to any details. This led Kahn to believe that Berkowitz was simply messing with the crime writer and knew nothing of the murder of Perry or anyone else at Stanford.

Martinson and Terry remain adamant that Berkowitz knows something as he was documented to have been in nearby Minot Air Force base before he committed his own murders. Martinson showed Berkowitz a series of photographs from people who Terry believed was involved with Perry's murder. Berkowitz identified one of the men in the photo as someone he had met during his satanic cult meetings in Minot.

FOREVER COLD

Detectives were hoping that with advanced DNA technology and handprint databases they would get a lead on the who left behind the semen and bloody handprint.

To date, there are still no leads.

Arlis' parents would stay in contact with the Santa Clara Sheriff's Department for more than thirty years.

Eventually, however, the sheriffs would stop returning their calls.

Arlis Perry's murder remains unsolved.